Mushroom Growing

MUSHROOM GROWING

S. C. DEY

Agrobios (India)

Dedicated

To

Shri Subhasis Dey

Published by:
Agrobios (India)
Behind Nasrani Cinema
Chopasani Road, Jodhpur 342 002
Phone: 0291-2643993, Fax: 0291-642319

ISBN (HB) : 978-81-7754-013-0
ISBN (PB) : 978-81-7754-271-4

Published by **Agrobios (India)**, Jodhpur
Lasertypeset at Yashee Computers, Jodhpur
Cover design by Reena
Printed at Babloo Offset, Jodhpur

Preface

Mushrooms are protein-rich-wonder food. They are delicious as well as nutritious. In past, its cultural techniques of the were not so improved. At present the modern techniques are more scientific which has assured more production because mushroom growing is not a difficult proposition Mushroom, unlike other crops, need no soil for its successful culture.. In India, the largest quantity is being grown in Himachal Pradesh. India has potential market of Mushroom, therefore, this text was prepared for general public as well for industrialists and scientists.

The text includes the important chapters like, History, Progress an India, Botanical Features and Propagation, Conventional Types of Compost, Compost Making and Spawning, Controlling, Weed Fungi, Temperature Requirements, Accessories and Equipment, Cultivation of Button Mushroom, Cultivation of Oyester Mushroom, Growing Paddy-Straw Mushroom, Preparing Grain Spawn, Do's and Dont's of Mushroom Growing, Delicious Recipes of Mushroom, Commercial Aspects and Economics, Nutrition From Mushroom, Mushroom Growing in Gardens, Preservation of Mushroom, Edible Mushrooms of this Country, Poisonous Mushrooms, Other Uses of Mushroom. The book also contains Appendices – Panaroma, Sources of Spawn, Bibliography and Scientific papers.

Horticultural Arena
Jhargram, 721507

S. C. DEY

MUSHROOM GROWING

S. C. Dey

About Book

Mushroom should no longer be identified with the scornful term, 'Toad-stool'. Now it is regarded as a protein-rich-wonder food and is no less useful than other indispensable fungi like yeast, *Penicillium*, *Streptomyces,* etc. The role of yeast is to cause fermentation for making malt, bread, alcohol etc. The fungus *Penicillium* is the source of the life-saving antibiotic penicillin. The antibiotic streptomycin to cure tuberculosis is obtained from streptomyces. The remedy of the deadly disease cancer is likely to be discovered in fungi. 'agerick' the universal remedy for all diseases and ailments is produced from a fungus, *Polyporus officinalis*. All these have created a furore to exploit mushroom which is going to bring about a revolution in the sphere of nutritive food and efficacious medicine.

The popularity of mushroom has grown since the time of the Greek and Roman civilizations. But the literature on its culture was first written in France during the reign of the great emperor Louis XIV (1638-1715).

The modern agro-technique of mushroom along with other related topics have been presented by the able and distinguished rosarian and horticulturist S.C. Dey in this book.

Publishers

Contents

Introduction

Mushroom, a protein-rich-wonder food needs more publicity as it deserves. It is then this precious vegetable would solve the problem of protein malnutrition in our country. Though there are more than 20 species in the list of edible mushrooms of the country there are only three which are considered promising in respect of commercial culture. These are white button mushroom, paddy-straw and oyester mushroom. Of them the former has gained the universal importance due to its delicacy as a food and rich contents of nutrition. In the northern parts of the country mushroom can be grown even in winter. For the normal growth of mycelium the day temperature should be 25- 26 °C. The pin heads that develop from the mycelium need the temperature of 16-19 °C.

The cultural techniques of the old days were not so improved, and for this reason the rate of production could not be controlled. But the modern techniques are more scientific, that has assured more production. Mushroom is delicious as well as nutritious. Its use as a food article in this country is from the time immemorial. But they were obtained as one of the natural vegetations, i.e. not grown as a crop as is done at present. Like other developed countries in India also the button mushroom is grown widely.

Mushroom growing is not a difficult proposition. But the compost prepared for growing mushroom may be infected with the disease-causing fungi which retard the growth of the crop. To get over the trouble the pasteurized compost is being used to grow button mushroom. This improved technique is simpler than the common practice and has been proved indispensable for the commercial culture. In this method the compost making has two parts. The first part comprising the works done outdoors. The second part is done indoors, which comprises the sterilization work by subjecting the compost to hot steam. For the domestic culture this expensive method is not feasible. But to be sure as to the high rate of production it is imperative. With a view to supplying sterilized compost to the farmers and the domestic growers a project was first undertaken in this country by UNDP in 1982 in Solan. In the next stage it was extended in Chail, Kanthaghat, Bangalore and Ootacamund. At present under the Indo-Dutch project the distribution of pasteurized compost among the farmers of Palampur (Himachal Pradesh), Jeolkote (U. P.), Srinagar (J & K), Bangalore (Karnatak) has been undertaken. It is encouraging that some business organisations have also come forward to help the farmers in this venture. They have arranged to supply the sterilized compost mixed with spawn to the farmers. Their activities are at present centered at the suburbs of the cities where the demand of mushroom has grown immensely.

In this country mushroom is grown in the largest quantity in Himachal Pradesh. There is an organisation named NCMRT made a survey to sort out the problems faced by the farmers. The more mushroom will be popular the more facilities will be extended to the farmers for its intensive and extensive culture. It is doubtless that those facilities are urgent in the interest of the prospective growers and farmers which are millions in number.

Mushroom, unlike other crops, need no soil for its successful culture. Gradually with the innovation of the improved cultural practices mushroom growing has been simplified. Now it is grown in the room with doors and windows. The temporary sheds on the roof top can be used with advantage for this purpose.

The remaining problems if sorted out mushroom growing will earn the status of an industry. In many villages of Haryana mushroom growing has been so extensive that it is regarded as an industry. There of course few voluntary organisations as well as government departments that has extended their help by supplying sterilized compost together with mushroom spawn to the farmers and the cottage scale growers.

As a natural vegetation mushroom grows in the forest, semi-forest or on the follow lands. Most of them are edible, which are collected and sold in the local markets. They are also seen growing in the shady corner of the large gardens especially under the shade of the large trees. By providing favourable condition their production can be controlled to some extent. Some of them are very delicious and comparable to button mushroom, the universally popular species. If humus and spawn are added to a fallow land under the shade of a tree the natural production can be increased, which has been discussed in the relevant chapter. One of them is *Agaricus campestris* which is grown by the author in his garden and a photograph of the same has been reproduced in this book for illustration. The pin heads and fruit bodies of the species are collected from the forest and sold in the market, the photograph of which has also been reproduced for the better understanding.

The book is written in the popular style of writing a technical subject. To reinforce the text a number of figures drawn by the author have been incorporated in this book along with some colour photographs. For all these the book claims a distinction and is considered to be useful to the readers.

History

Carlyle says, Nature alone is antique and the oldest art a mushroom'. This suggests that mushroom is associated with the antiquity. An interesting story referring to mushroom is found in Alice in Wonderland. The story relates a mushroom one side of which if eaten the man will grow tall instantaneously. When the other side of it is tasted the extra height will be reduced, thus maintaining status quo.

On studying the plant science we have come to know that in the process of evolution algae came first, which was followed by fungi. The relevant sub-division of the science is *Mycology* which comprises all aspects including the life cycle of this group of plants. There is a term *myke* in the Greek mythology, which refers to something having a cap-like structure. Obviously a large group of fungi including mushrooms has a dome-like structure on a stalk-like stem. In *Rigveda,* we have come across *Somarasa-* a strongly stimulated drink. It has been discovered that it was prepared from the extract of *Amanita muscaria* a well-known mushroom species. *Somarasa* was a sacred drink which was offered to God by the Aryans in the occasions of worship and *Jajna.* The modern researchers have come to know that the one of the ingredients of preparing Somarasa is the extract of a mushroom. The name of Wasson (G. R. Wasson, 1969) an American research worker is associated with this work. In Guatemala mushroom is found in the pre-historic cave paintings and engraved on the cave walls. In Mesopotamea mushroom is esteemed as one of the objects of offering to gods and goddesses. This has been presumed by the knowledgeable persons from the ancient paintings and other works of engraving, sculpturing etc. In all ancient civilizations various ornaments were designed with the replica of mushroom. In some postage stamps of Bulgaria the prints of mushroom is found. In all parts of ancient Europe mushroom enjoyed the royal prerogatives. Because it was esteemed as one of the main articles of the royal luxury.

When the glory of Raman Empire was at its peak all the luxury articles of the highest value were collected from the wide world for the Roman emperors. Roman historian Piny (AD 23-AD 79) writes in his natural History that two species of mushroom (*Amanita caesaria* and *Boletus eludis*) were regarded as a great delicacy and as such was eaten in the plates of a precious metal. Not only in Rome alone in all parts of Europe also mushroom were regarded as the luxury goods by the people of the highest social order. There was a peculiar code of law in the continent of the middle ages (1100-1400 AD) which governed the aristocracy implicitly. The law would control the movements of the domestic animals. The pets like dogs, pigs, bears etc. were employed to find out mushroom from the forest land for the royals and the nobles. In those days though mushroom was regarded as a good food article its cultivation might have been in vogue to some extent; but no mention of it was found in black and white. The writing of mushroom culture was started in the reign of Louis XIV the great emperor of France (1638--1715). But first scientific literature was written in French by Turnifort and was published in 1707. The first learnt its culture from the growth of mushroom on the heap of decomposed rice husk and straw which was used by them for manuring the orchards. Many attractive species of mushroom would grow on the piles of plant residues. In the later period the French mushroom specialists and mycologists innovated the improved cultural practices which were being followed till today.

The English learnt the mushroom culture from the French people very rapidly. In the early decades of the twentieth century they would collect the natural spawn of mushroom and export to the countries like America, Germany, Denmark and Australia. By the end of nineteenth century two French mycologists, Matrocot and Constantina (1894) had been able to remove the two impediments of mushroom culture through research works. First they used the sulphur fumigation as a remedy for the disease of La moul (*Mycogona perniciosa*). The second being the invention of growing sterile spawn after germinating the mushroom spores, that contributes to extending the mushroom culture scientifically. Though the technique was patented but it was not exploited commercially , In 1902, Miss Ferguson of Crone explained the technique of germinating the spores broadly. In 1905, American scientist Duggar invented the pure call suspension culture from the mushroom tissue. Immediately the technique created a furore among the mushroom growers. Because this process ensures the production of pure spawn of a particular strain. Needless to say, this raised the mushroom culture to the status of an industry in the developed countries.

In 1918, Lambert in America produced the pure culture spawn in the glass bottles and began to sell to the mushroom growers. The technique was to germinate the spores in a sterilized condition and then to inject them into the bottle of sterilized compost prepared from horse dung. During the fourth decade of the present century a greenhouse suitable for growing mushroom throughout the year was innovated that could control the humidity, temperature and ventilation suitable for the culture easily. The French farmers understood that the role of plaster of Paris to make the compost friable and granular is very important. In 1936, Piger observed that the gypsum (Plaster of Peris, $CaSO_4$) in the compost is indispensable, because it stimulates the growth of mycelium very rapidly. Sinden discovered the use of grain in making spawn in 1932 and patented the technique. During the second World War the agricultural department of America declared that mushroom is very rich in nutrition and at the same time its culture compete well with any popular vegetable in regard to the demand of the land, fertilizer and irrigation etc. In the middle of this century the Mushroom Growers Association was set up in England and Ireland. It conducted the research works to solve the problems of mushroom culture as a specialist branch of the National Farmers Union. And then the Midland Group of publication was established that published the standard books and periodicals to improve the industry of mushroom culture. Afterwards, the technique of growing mushroom in polybags was innovated which became very popular among domestic growers. The mushroom culture spread widely with the introduction of Benlate to remove the disease of mushroom. Now the leading countries in mushroom growing are Japan, Korea, Italy and Malay.

Progress In India

In 1886 mushroom culture was exhibited by N. W. Newton in the annual exhibition held in the garden of the Horticultural Society of India (Calcutta). In 1908 Sir David Prain undertook the work of extensive investigation as to the edible mushroom in India. Because he observed that the poor people of the famine-striken area of this country lived with mushroom as their subsistence. In 1962 Indian Science Congress met in Nagpur. There a scientist named S. R Basu expounded the sterilized compost from horse dung invented by him for growing mushroom. Moreover he hold the view that the mushroom growing in India can be a potential industry. In 1941, Padwick remarked that though button mushroom (*A. biporus*) was successfully grown in most of the countries of the world it did not show any progress in India. So he uphold the potentiality and pointed out the impediments of the culture of button mushroom in this country.

In the period between 1939-1945 the agricultural department under the Government of Madras began the investigation into the culture of the species *Volvariella* spp. Thomas and his associates presented the details of the culture of *Volvariella*. In 1947, Asthana used flour of gram in the growing medium of *Volvariella* and succeeded in having more production. He told that the best period of growing this species in Madhya Pradesh being April-June. Besides he had been able to give the chemical analysis of mushroom. In 1961, under the auspices of Indian Council of Agricultural Research the Agricultural Department of Himachal Pradesh took up a large project to improve the mushroom culture in the State. In the first stage the use of cow manure as a medium was tried. But it was proved not to be good. Then experiments were made with the use of stable manure and the success was achieved. Then for the commercial purpose wheat straw, chemical fertilizers and some organic substances were used for making compost. This compost was known as 'Synthetic compost'. Then 'casing' was invented to cover the compost after spawning. The casing materials were mixed with insecticide and fungicide that created a great interest among the growers. This type of casing protects the medium from disease and insect attacks resulting in more production.

First the commercial culture of mushroom was started in Delhi and Solan, and then it spread to Jammu and Kashmir, Nilgiri, Punjab, Haryana, Chandigarh, Uttar Pradesh, Maharastra, Madhya Pradesh and Gujrat. In 1982, under the 6th five-year plan Indian Council of Agricultural Research sanctioned the fund for setting up a organisation named National Centre for Mushroom Research and Training (NCMRT). The objective was to sort out the problems of mushroom culture and to arrange training for the scientific workers, teachers, demonstrators and extension workers. Simultaneously All India Co-ordinated Mushroom Improvement Project was also set up. Under this organisation two centres started the research works on the regional basis. The first centre started its work in 1983 in Solan (Himachal Pradesh).

Botanical Features and Propagation

The most species of fungus is minute or microscopic. The group of the largest species being the mushroom. All fungi are divided into two groups - useful and harmful species. One of the most useful fungus is *Penicillium* from which the well-known antibiotic *penicillin* is produced. Yeast is also a very useful fungus that has extensive uses in making malt, wine and bread. The solution of sugar with water if left for hours yeast will grow in it and through the process of fermentation alcohol and carbon dioxide will be produced. But in the presence of more oxygen the quantity of alcohol will decrease. In the rainy season yeast grow in molasses and due to fermentation it emits the scent of a liquor. The sweet fruits if cut and left for hours yeast will grow in it. If the syrup of *Rosogolla* (a popular sweet of Bengal) is not concentrated enough yeast will grow in it and cause fermentation. But yeast cannot grow in the strongly concentrated sugar solution, say above 75 per cent. For this reason the concentrated sugar solution serves as a preservative for many sweets, pickles and fruit preserves.

The harmful fungi are numerous. Many diseases of plants and animals are caused by fungi, e.g., late blight of potato is caused by a fungus *Phytopthora infestans*. The rust of wheat is caused by *Puccinia graminis* which is a fungus. The mildews of plants are fungous diseases.

Obviously the fungi are plants but do not possess chlorophyll, the green colouring matter. Hence the direct sunlight is not indispensable to them for manufacturing their own food. Fungus is non-flowering, so cannot bear fruits. Instead it bears spores that serve as seed. When the plant parts begin to decompose fungi grow on them, obtain their food and multiply. The fungus has no roots. It has a root-like appendage (mycelium) that grow under the ground or substrate and serve the purpose of roots. The spores germinate to grow hypha. Then the hypha grows to from a net-like spreading structure which is called 'mycelium'. It forms the pin heads or fruit bodies. In case of the large fungi the fruit body is known as 'mushroom'.

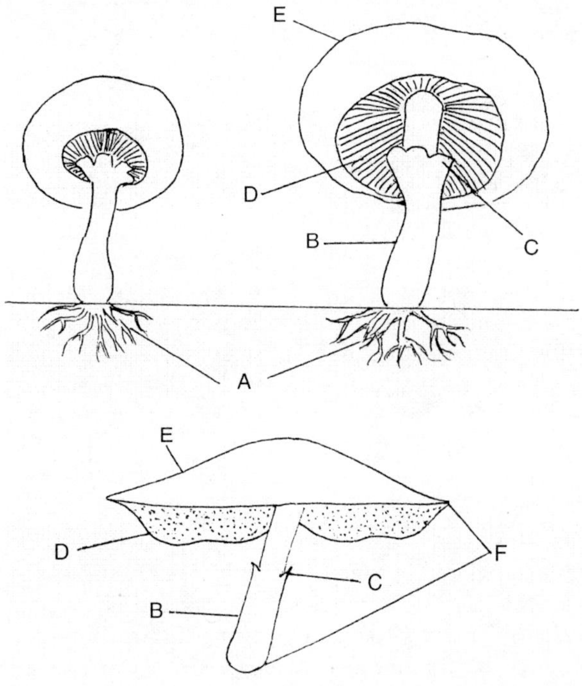

Fig 1: Different parts of mushroom, A. Mycelium, B. Stipe, C. Veil, D. Gill, E. Pileus, F. Longitudinal section

The most of the large fungi belong to the family Agaricaceae, e.g., *Agricus bisporus* (Button mushroom). It is an edible mushroom. Some of the edible mushrooms are grown like vegetables.

Habitat and Morphology

Agricus campestris is a common mushroom which grows like a saprophyte in the fields, pastures and open fallow lands close to the forest. The land with a thin forest crops is very suitable for this species but is never found in a dense forest as well as in coniferous forests. As it is edible we take it as vegetable. It can be grown near the trees or shrubs of the garden. Its mycelium is perennial that grows in the sub-soil. Gradually it spreads horizontally. But for its growth it needs more humus in the subsoil, which is generally supplied by the rotting roots of the shrub-like weeds or other vegetations.

Generally in September and October the temperature and humidity attain a level which is conducive to forming sporophore or pin head. The pin heads pass through the deep soil layer and raise their heads above the ground and spread an umbrella-like head.

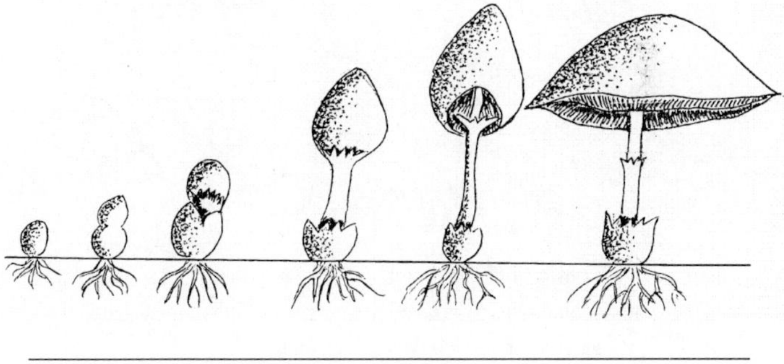

Fig. 2: The gradual growth of mushroom

The mycelium of A. *campestris* is perennial, which consists of branch-like spreading colourless hyphae. The cells of hypha contain granular vacuole and protoplasm with many nuclei and oil drops. These serve as food for the fungus. The hyphae of A. *campestris* are not connected with each other, i.e. they remain separated but very close to each other.

The immature sporophores are round and dilated. In this stage the sporophore is known as 'button'. A mature sporophore has two parts - (A) Stipe that looks like stem or stalk. On the upper part of the stripe has a ring (Veil) encirling it, B - pileus that grows like an umbrella on the top of the stipe. The border of the Pileus remains attached to the ring of the stipe in the early stage. In the first stage the pileus is convex, then it gradually becomes flat. The colour of the pileus may be white, off white, grey or brown. The periphery of the pileus may be wavy or serrated. The central portion is fleshy.

There are innumerable thin plate like appendages extending from the from the stipe to the border of the pileus is called gills. They are however free from the stipe. on maturity the gills become purple brown to chocolate brown.

The spores grow on the gills. A minute organ named *basidium (sing.)* grows on gills, which produce spores on its head. Basidia are actually spore-mother cells. On maturity the spores are detached and dispersed from the basidia (*pl*). In a favourable condition, the spores are germinated to from one or more hyphae. They inturn, grow into mycelium.

Fig. 3: Mycelium from a germinated spore. A. Hypha is grown from a spore, B. Mycelium from hrpha, C. Pin heads and fruit bodies grown from mycelium.

In mushroom culture for artificial propagation spores are collected. A process named 'paper print' has been innovated and by this process the plenty of spores can be collected easily. A colour photograph has been reproduced for illustration, and the process has been described in Chapter 12 with figures.

The following are the few species of mushroom which are grown and used as vegetable.

1. *Agaricus bisporus* (white button mushroom).
2. *Phellorinia inquinaus* (*Rumbhi*).
3. *Pleurotus sajor* - caju (*Dhingri*).
4. *Volvariella volvacca* (Paddy-straw mushroom, Poal chhatu).

Conventional Types of Compost

For growing *Agaricus bisporus* a special type of compost is required which can be used for growing garden plants. But *Volvariella* spp and *A. bisporus* need different types of medium.

For the culture of *A. bisporus* some specific nutrients are required which are available in a good number of materials and they are used in making compost. Though the ingredients differ in the different mixtures the resultant nutritional value being almost the same. The availability of the ingredients are regional. Therefore, if only one mixture is recommended all of their ingredients may not be procurable locally. So for the sake of choice a number of mixtures are formulated and mentioned below.

1 Wheat straw.. 1000 kg.
Poultry manure .... 400 kg.
Wheat bran (*Bhusi*) .... 25 kg.
Urea .... 14.5 kg.
Gypsum (Calcium sulphate, $CaSO_4$)................. 30 kg.

The mixture has been recommended by the National Centre for Mushroom Research and Training (Solan, Himachal Pradesh). The farmers of the village of Bhadana near Solan produce button mushroom using this compost.

2 Paddy straw.. 500 kg.
Horse manure (stable manure) .... 100 kg.
Poultry manure.. 300 kg.
Wheat bran.. 12.5 kg.
Urea .... 7 kg.
Gypsum (plaster of paris).................................. 30 kg.

The mixture is recommended by the University of Horticulture and Foresty of Solan. By using this compost the many farmers of Chail, Simla, Manali, Khoradhara etc. of Himachal Pradesh are producing white button mushroom in quantities.

3 Wheat straw (1" - 4" long chips) .... 300 kg.
Wheat bran.. 15 kg.
Calcium ammoniam nitrate (CAN)................. 6 kg.
Urea .... 2.5 kg.
Super phosphate .... 7.5 kg.
Gypsum (calcium sulphate).............................. 30 kg.

This mixture is recommended by Indian Council of Agricultural Research.

4 Wheat straw (8-20 cm. long chips).................. 300 kg.
Wheat bran.. 30 kg.
Urea .... 4 kg.
Ammonium sulphate... 9 kg.
Super phosphate .... 2 kg.
Potassium sulphate .... 3 kg.
Gypsum .... 30 kg.

This quantity of compost can be sufficient for filling 20--22 trays. This is too recommended by Indian Council of Agricultural Research.

5 Paddy straw.. 100 kg.
Ammonium sulphate... 18 kg.
Urea .... 4.5 kg.
Super phosphate .... 18 kg.
Quick lime (CaO) .... 27 kg.

This simple formula is innovated by the scientist of Taiwan (Ho).

Compost Making and Spawning

The compost making demands earnestness and carefulness on the part of the farmers. All details should be followed meticulously.

COMPOST

Ingredients	Quantity
1. Wheat straw/paddy straw (1" - 4" long)	300 kg.
2. Wheat bran	15 kg.
3. Cal. Am. Nitrate (CAN)	6 kg.
4. Urea	2.5 kg.
5. Super phosphate	7.5 kg.
6. Potassium sulphate	3 kg.
7. Gypsum	30 kg.

Mix the ingredients of 3-6 nos. with 5 kg. of saw dust. Before mixing get the saw dust moist. Heap the mixture for a day so that the chemicals are mixed well with the saw dust. Next day soak the straw chips. First spread the chips on a cemented floor, then sprinkle water with a water can. Then spread the fertilizer mix and wheat bran on the soaked straw and mix them well.

Pile the mixture for decomposition. The width and height of the stack should be 150 m. The length is obviously dependant on the amount of the material. Cover the stack with a sheet of polythene.

Within 3-4 days the fermentation will start in the pile and consequently the temperature will rise to 60-80 °C.

Compost will be prepared when the process of decomposition will be completed which will take 28-30 days. In this period the pile has to be broken for aeration and piled again as before. This process has to be repeated at least thrice. Each time if some amount of extra manure is added the quality of the compost will be much improved. A mixture of the following ingredients may be used for this purpose.

Wheat bran.. 15 kg.
CAN (Calcium ammonium nitrate) .... 3 kg.
Urea .... 1 kg.

Mix CAN and urea with the moist wheat barn and keep overnight. This can be applied when the stack is broken for the second time. Before piling, apply water by sprinkling to remove the shortage of moisture. For this use a water can fitted with its fine rose. Care should be taken to sprinkle water uniformly. Water in excess will be harmful. Have a pinch of compost and squeeze between the two fingers. If water oozes out take it for granted that watering has been more. Follow the work schedule given below.

First day	Mixing fertilizers with straw chips.
Sixth day	The stack is broken and oiled again for aeration.
Tenth day	The stack is broken.

Second time, some extra manure is mixed with it before piling again. Then on every third day the stack should be broken for aeration and piled again as before. If the moisture level goes down sprinkle water before piling. This process will be continued for 25 days. Whether the compost has been prepared that can be tasted easily. On the age of 28 days if the foul gas of ammonia does not evolve from the stack the compost has been ready for use. If not, a few days more might be required.

This is another process of compost making using the third mixture of the preceding chapter.

Soak the straw chips with water on a cemented floor. Then mix the full amount of wheat bran (15 kg.) and half of the fertilizer mixture together.

Heap the mixture in a space of one square metre. Care should be taken to see that the pile should remain uniformly moist. The stack should not be disturbed for a week. Because the fermentation will start in this period and consequently the temperature will rise within the stack. After a week the stack should be broken, the rest of the manure should be mixed and piled again as before. The materials of the surface layer of the stack are subjected to less fermentation. For this reason it will be put in the middle of the stack at the time of next piling. To maintain the required moisture level sprinkling water may be needed. The full quantity of gypsum (30 kg) will be divided into three and each portion should be used in each time of breaking of the stack. When the compost will be ready its colour will be black, the condition will be moist and smell will not be foul, rather sweet like that of fresh hay. If not so, it is yet to be decomposed, and a few days more might be required.

The scientist P. K. Seth of the Agriculture University of Himachal Pradesh writes that there are processes for growing button mushroom-one is short and other is long. The short-termed process is suitable for the commercial purpose. Because this process involves the pasteurization of the compost that always ensures the high level of production. For sterilizing compost the equipment for applying steam at a high pressure is required. But for the domestic growers the compost that can be used without making germ-free has also been recommended. Now a long process of making compost will be discussed here. The ingredients are as follows.

1 Wheat straw (cuttings of 8--20 cm. long) .... 300 kg.

2 Wheat bran .... 30 kg.

3 Urea .... 5 kg.

4 Ammonium sulphate .... 9 kg.

5 Super phosphate .... 2 kg.

6 Potassium sulphate /wood ash .... 3 kg.

7 Gypsum .... 30 kg.

Soak the straw chips in water for two days. To do this spread the materials with a uniform thickness on a cemented floor. Then sprinkle water with a water can at an interval of few hours.

Mix the ingredients of the numbers 3--6 with the half of wheat bran (15 kg.) and add a little water to moisten the mixture pile the mixture and cover the pile with a hessian cloth. Next day this mixture is to be mixed with wet straw cuttings. Stack the mixture as usual.

THE WORK SCHEDULE

- **First day (1) :** Spread the wet straw cuttings on a cemented floor, scatter the mixture of wheat bran and other chemicals over it uniformly and all the ingredients will be mixed thoroughly. Then pile the mixture in a rectangular stack (1.8 m long, 1.5 m breadth and 1.5 m height). Within 48 hours the temperature inside the stack will rise above 60 °C due to fermentation. 6th day (2) : Though the material inside the stack begins to decompose, that of the surface layer exposed to air remains intact. Separate the undigested material of 15 cm. deep of the surface layer and sprinkle water to soak it. Break the stack and mix the two lots together thoroughly, and add to it 30 kg. of CAN or ammonium sulphate, 3 kg. of urea and the remaining 15 kg. of wheat bran. Of course, before mixing the chemical fertilizer and wheat bran they are mixed and kept in a moist condition for 24 hours. Then stack the mixture as before. This time a little insecticide (0.5 g) like Furadan 3G should be mixed with the compost material. On 10th day (3): Separate the undigested material of the surface layer and get it moistened. Break the stack and mix both the materials together thoroughly and pile again as before.

- **On 13th days (4) :** Follow the same as is done on the 10th day. But only exception is to add 30 kg. of gypsum to the decomposing material. Sprinkle water as needed. It is again said that the excess water is harmful. Take a pinch of the material and squeeze it between the fingers. If water oozes take it for granted that water has been added more than what is needed.

- **On 16th day (5) :** Break the pile and stack again.

- **On 19th day (6) :** The same as before.

- **On 22th day (7) :** The same as before.

- **On 25th day (8) :** The same as before.

- **On 28th day (9) :** Break the stack and check the smell. If ammonia gas is still generated stack again for a few days.

Watering the compost stack is to be done carefully. Water just to make it moist. On watering the mixture of straw cuttings and the fertilizer mix water should not spill out. Because with the spilling water certain amount of fertilizer is lost.

A simple method of compost making innovated in 1978 by a Taiwan scientist Ho is given below.

Paddy-straw cuttings	1000 kg.
Ammonium sulphate	18 kg.
Urea	4.5 kg.
Super phosphate	18 kg.
Quick lime (CaO)	27 kg.

Soak the straw cutting in water on a cemented floor. Then add the other ingredients and pile the mixture as usual. Cover the stack with a sheet of polythene. On the fourth day break the stack for aeration and pile it again as before. The process has to be repeated thrice on the 8th day, 12th day and the 16th day. After 20 days the trays will be filled with the compost. And it is then the compost is ready for spawning.

The quantity of water added to the compost greatly influences the mushroom production. If more water is added the nutrients will be leached out, and the quality of the compost will be poor. If the heap is too dry it will not complete decomposition and create problems for the mushroom growth.

The water content of the compost should necessarily be 68 per cent, which can be determined by a simple test. Squeeze a pinch of compost in-between the two fingers. On hard pressing if the droplets ooze it is be understood that the desired moisture level has been attained.

SPAWNING

Properly prepared compost is put in the trays and then spawn is added to it. The trays may be made of wood, plastic of fibre glass. The size and shape of the trays has been discussed in the relevant chapter.

Fill the trays with compost to the rim. The mycelium of mushroom is treated as mushroom seed or spawn. In the laboratory the mycelium is grown in the medium of sorghum starch and put into bottles. The farmers have to procure these spawn bottles and the mycelium growing therein is taken out and added to the compost. Now mushroom spawn is available from the business firms, regional govt. laboratories, agricultural universities etc. Some voluntary organisations have come forward to extend their services for spreading mushroom culture. They distribute viable mushroom spawn among the farmers under their command area.

The spawn contained in a half-litre bottle is sufficient to spawn the compost of three trays. If the spawn bottles are not used preserve the bottles. At the 4 °C of a refrigerator the spawn in bottles can be preserved well.

The spawn is taken out after breaking the bottle. Scatter the spawn uniformly over the compost of the tray. Then push them into the compost with the finger tips. It however should not go below the depth of 5 cm. Then cover the trays with news paper. To soak the paper water is sprinkled over it. The trays are stacked in a well-ventilated room. How they will be stacked has been described and illustrated in the relevant chapter. The temperature of the room should be 24-25 °C. It will take 12--15 days to spread the mycelium in the entire mass of the compost. If the room temperature goes below 24 °C the mycelium growth will be retarded. Care should be taken to see that the paper cover should always remain moist. Therefore sprinkling of water is needed at a regular interval. When the surface of the compost is covered with the mycelium growth remove the paper cover. Overspread a layer (2-3 cm. thickness) of clay paste. Pure clay should not be used as it will prevent aeration. Mix some leaf mould with light loam. To give it a paste-like consistency add water as needed. The porosity of the material is high, which will facilitate aeration and percolation of water applied by spraying. The covering of clay is termed as 'Casing'. The casing material should be sterilized before use. Theat one cubic metre of the soil mixture with three litre of one per cent solution of formalin. This quantity of soil is sufficient for casing 60--70 trays. Within a few days after casing the pin heads for fruit bodies will break the soil cover and raise their heads through it.

Controlling Weed Fungi

As the weed growth redards the growth of the garden plants the weed mould grown in the compost impedes the growth of mushroom. Not only the quantity but also quality of the crop is affected, which is reflected in the appearances of the fruit bodies. The crooked forms of the fruit bodies indicate the presence of the weed mould in the compost. Many types of mould are found to grow on the organic substances. For example, the cotton garments soaked in perspiration are very susceptible to the mould growth in a humid environment. The reed mats if kept rolled in the rainy season the mould will grow on their surfaces. We are used to seeing the mould growth on curds or stale foods. Similarly orange peels in moist weather are attacked by the mould. But this fungus is very well-known and useful to us. It is Penicilium from which antibiotic like *Penicillin* is prepared. This *penicilium* may grow in the compost as a mould. Other species of fungus that grow as weed moulds in the compost are mentioned below.

Needless to say, for the quality growth of mushroom the compost must be weed-free. It has been already mentioned that the high crop yield is ensured if the compost is sterilized by subjecting it to high-pressure steam. But this costly method is hardly applicable by the domestic growers. To achieve the end they cannot but take precautions to some extent. In many parts of the country sterilized compost is distributed among the small farmers by the government organisations. Now it is imperative to extend the facility by the agricultural department to the farmers of the other parts also. If the species of the mould is identified the defect of the compost can be sorted out. For example, if there is the mould of *Coprinus* spp. it is to be understood that much of ammonia gas has evolved. And in this condition *Oedocephalum* species also may grow. In making compost a definite ratio of carbon and nitrogen has to be maintained. It so happens that in most cases the quantity of carbon outweighs that of nitrogen. In such condition a mould of *Tricoderma* species is found to grow. It is commonly known as *green mould*. It grows when the quantity of carbon becomes more than that of nitrogen. Carbon is derived from carbohydrates. The major part of the compost contains straw and bran, the main constituents of them being carbohydrates. If the quantity of nitrogen is less the digestion of straw and wheat bran will be delayerd. It is then carbon becomes more in quantities than nitrogen. If carbohydrates are partially decomposed simple sugars are released, which favours the growth of grey whiker mould (*Doratomyces microsporus*). Besides *Aspergillus* and *Penicilium* moulds may grow.

If aminos are deposited by the disintegration of protein certain species of mould grow which are *Thielavia therimorphila*, *Sporobolomyces* spp and *Trichothecium roseum*. In common parlance they are known as 'White Plaster Mould'. If in the first stage ingredients of compost are digested rapidly and in the later stage if proper attention is not paid to the compost white plaster mould is likely to grow.

If the pH value of the compost diminishes, i.e. the acidity increases the deficiency of oxygen will occur. Then those bacteria which do not need oxygen will be growing in the compost. But the lack of oxygen does not favour the growth of mould. But the bacteria indirectly help produce mould. Because they through metabolism produce certain metabolites which are helpful to the growth of weed mould. Those moulds appear in the last stage when the fruit bodies raise their heads through the clay plaster (casing). This mould is known as *Olive green mould* (*Chaelomium olivaceum*).

Due to excess moisture in the compost a mould named *Brown Plaster Mould* (*Populaspora byssina*) grows. This mould may grow even in pasteurized compost if poly-bags are used instead of the trays as the containers. Because poly-bags help to increase the stagnant moisture. If the moisture level of the compost is high the mycelium will be thin. If poly-bags are used the moisture of the compost should be less. In other words if the percentage of moisture is 66, that for the poly-bags it should be 63.

Temperature Requirements

In our plains mushroom can be grown throughout the year. In the northern plains where winter is long and intensity of cold is high mushroom is grown through all seasons. In the coldest region of Kashmir mushroom is being grown in winter. In this regard the views of different scientists are laid down here.

The growth of mushroom is completed in two stages. The first stage comprises the growth of mycelium and in the second stage fruit bodies develop from them. The fruit bodies come above the compost whereas the mycelium grow like the roots in the compost. For the optimum production the temperature requirements for the growth of mycelium and the growth of pin heads are different. Dr. S. L. Katyal, the Director General of ICAR writes in one of his articles that for the growth of mycelium 25 °C is highly suitable. But for the growth of pin heads 16-18 °C is most congenial. This temperature refers to the day temperature which may come down at night. If there is no arrangement for controlling the temperature the crop can be grown in the recommended temperatures when available. But the production in a commercial scale demands no variation in the requisite temperature. Therefore the arrangement for controlling temperature must be there. D. K. Chakraborty and B. B. Sarker of Bhidhan Chandra Krishi Viswavidyalaya have written in an article that mushroom can be grown in the temperature from 20-30 °C. J. N. Kapoor and Nita Bahl working under ICAR mention in an article that for the good growth of white button mushroom the temperature requirement being 23-26 °C. Neelam Chabra of the same organisation writes in her article that white button mushroom grows well from October to February when the day temperatures varies from 16-18 °C. In case of a high temperature, the air cooler can be used to lower the temperature.

Accessories and Equipment

The first requirement being a cemented floor outside the house. The water requirement is considerable for making compost. Compost has to be prepared under a shed. If the shed is not available suitable polythene sheets are required to protect the compost from the sun and shower.

After spawing the winged insects must be kept at bay. Therefore the windows should be fitted with the mosquito netting. The ventillation of the room should be normal. If a verandah is used for this purpose it should be enclosed by nylon mosquito netting.

TRAY BEDS

It is easy to grow mushroom in trays, wooden or plastic. Many trays can be kept arranged in a small space. In a stack 7-8 rows of trays one above the other can be kept. All the trays should necessarily be the same in shape and size. Generally the dimensions should be 100cm × 50cm × 15cm. Between the two adjacent stacks a passage of 60cm must be given as in the garden a path is allowed between the two beds, which is essential to perform the cultivation works.

Stack the trays vertically one over the other. The trays should be provided with the wooden pegs so as to leave enough space between the trays for various reasons such as watering, applying pesticides, air circulation and harvesting.

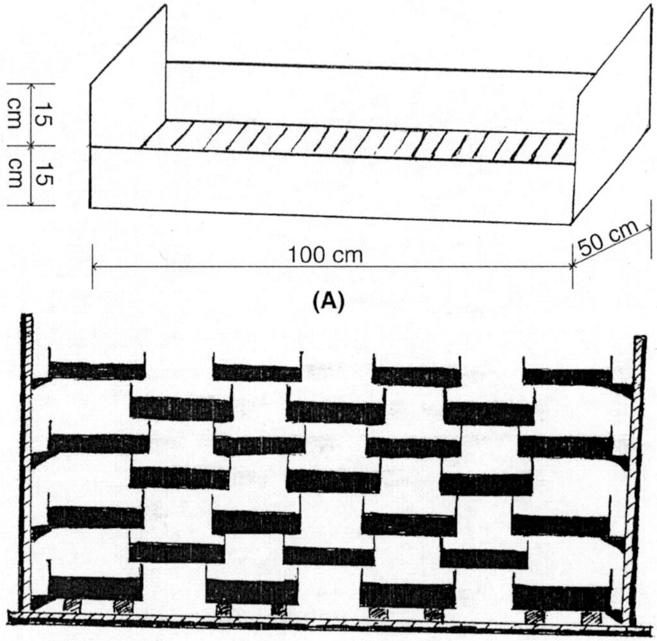

Fig. 4: Tray-beds for growing button mushroom. Trays are stacked one above the other, A - Design of a tray.

Cultivation of Button Mushroom

The Latin name of the button mushroom is *Agaricus bisporus*. If the factors on which its production is dependent are provided by the controlling measure its production is possible anywhere at any season. The related factors are the temperature, moisture, ventilation and seed (spawn). These are discussed separately hereunder.

Fig. 5: Button mushroom

TEMPERATURE

On spawing hyphae begin to grow. When they form a net work is called mycelium. This is the first phase of growth. In the second phase of growth fruit bodies or pin heads grow from the mycelium. The growth of these two phase requires two different temperatures. Hyphae and mycelium growth becomes optimum in the temperature of 20-25 °C. And the ideal temperature for the growth of pin heads is 14-18 °C. A wide fluctuation of this range of temperature is definitely harmful. If it goes down the growth of hyphae and pin heads will be impeded. On the contrary if it is increased weed mould will grow to cause the disease of mushroom.

White button mushroom can be grown in the hills at an altitude of 2000m for raising 5 crops in a year. It can be grown throughout the year in the places like Chail, Simla, Manali and Kheradhar without adopting artificial heating in winter. The list of the other places where it can be grown for the number of crops a year without heating facilities in winter is given below.

Places	No. of crops
Kasauli	3
Dalhousie	3
Dharmasala	3
Solan	2
Kotgarh	2
Palampur	2
Jagji Nagar	1
Nalagarh (H.P.)	1
Srinagar and its surroundings	2
Ladakh	3
Jammu region	2
Nainital	3-4
Almorah	3-4
Dehradun	2-3
Mussoorie	2-3
Nilgiri (S. India)	4-5
Pulney hills	4-5

Besides in the plains of India the suitable weather condition reaches with the advent of winter, i.e. from November to mid March.

HUMIDITY

The humidity of the environment and the moisture of the compost should be just as needed. The loss of moisture is harmful. The maximum humidity of the atmosphere is suitable for the growth of button mushroom. When the atmosphere becomes dry the humidity of the room can be increased by sprinkling water by sprayer or sprinkler. It should be borne in mind that watering the compost after spawing is not recommended. Therefore always maintain the optimum humidity of the room so that the compost does not tend to run dry.

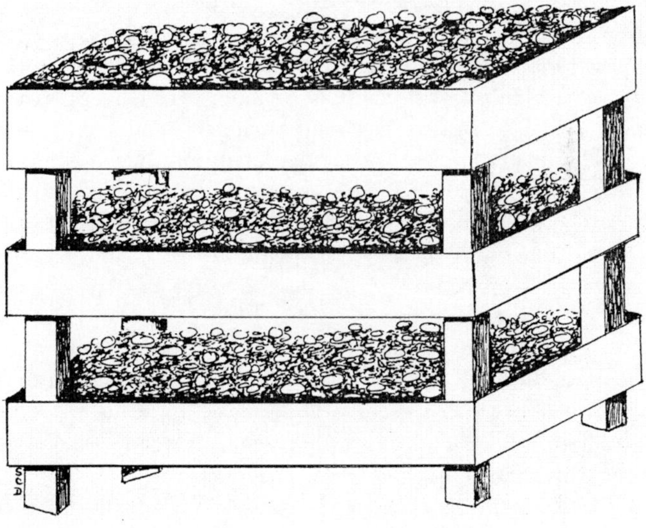

Fig. 6: mushroom grown on wooden shelves.

VENTILATION

The farmer has to reduce the presence of carbon dioxide in the room. To achieve this good ventilation of the room should be secured. Carbon dioxide should not rise above 0.15 per cent of the total volume of air in the room. The rise in the concentration of the gas (carbon dioxide) is definitely harmful to the normal growth of mushroom. It should be understood that for one degree rise in temperature above 16 °C carbon dioxide evolves 25 per cent more. Therefore with the rise in temperature the ventilation must be increased which will reduce the concentration of the harmful gas.

SPAWN

The grower must have a clear idea of the seed of mushroom. Though a fungus is a plant it does not bear flowers. So seed is not produced. Instead of seed spore is produced which is used, like seed, for propagation. The fern is a group of plants that does not bear flowers and fruits. Instead of it ferns produce spores in sporangiams on the under side of the leaflets. The spores of mushroom are finer than those of the fern. Mushroom seeds are actually the sterile mycelium grown in a sterilized cereal starch medium contained in a bottle. It is prepared in the laboratory and the bottles of spawn are sold to the farmers. If the supply is not at par with the demand a substitute can be used. The mycelium of the bed just after the harvest of the first batch can be used for spawning. The lumps of compost having more mycelium growth will be selected. They will be cut into pieces of small cubes and used as spawn immediately. The difference lies in that the laboratory spawn is pusteurized but the farmer's spawn is not so. Therefore it favours the growth of weed mould and as such it cannot be used for the commercial culture. But for the domestic culture sometimes one has to depend on the second line of supply that comes from his own beds. The specimen mushroom from which spawn will be produced in the laboratory should be of a particular species and of high quality. When the mycelium growth covers the entire mass of grain starch in the bottle that will be broken to take out the spawn for using in the compost beds. But if not well-pasteuriged the mycelium would not cover the entire mass uniformly. This indicates the presence of weed mould. The fresh mycelium and the fresh mushroom have the same smell. Therefore if the mycelium of the bottle is not dried it will emit the smell of a fresh mushroom. All these enable you to build up your understanding as to the quality spawn of mushroom

TIPS ON GROWING BUTTON MUSHROOM

Button mushroom is grown indoors

1. A verandah is better than a room as it does not create any problem of ventilation. Secondly bringing, handling and removing of the materials and accessories are convenient.

2. The direct sun should be obstructed. But the diffused sun does not affect the mushroom beds.

3. From spawning to harvesting the room temperature should not rise above 20 °C.

4. If the temperature comes down an arrangement should be there to control it artificially for maintaining the required temperature.
5. The humidity of the room should not rise to the optimum. If reached, the ventilation should be more than usual.
6. To disinfect the room the application of fumigant is necessary. The doors and windows should be closed during the fumigation. Therefore the room must have the well-fitted doors and windows and the ventilators with their shutters. The fumigation should be done just before the spawning.

The work schedule for growing button mushroom.

(i) Compost making by adopting correct methods.

(ii) Collecting quality spawn and spawning.

(iii) Casing the beds on spawning.

(iv) Harvesting (Picking fruit bodies).

MORE ABOUT THE CULTURE

The ingredients of a compost are many. The compost is used as a medium on which mushroom grows. The compost medium is known as *substrate*. The layer in which hyphae grows is called *substratum*. The main ingredients of a compost areorganic substances which are obtained as the wastes of plants and animals. As for example, grass, straw, hedge clippings, garbage, green manure, farmyard manure etc. Cattle dung when decomposed can be used as a substrate. Stable manure obtained from horse dung is considered better than cattle dung. The dung obtained from the cattle fed with more straw is considered better than the other dungs in this respect i.e. for making compost for mushroom.

Wheat straw is found better than paddy straw. Saw dust obtained from the wood sawing industry is a very good ingredient for making compost. The dust of hardwood is obviously better than that of soft wood. Because soft wood contains more resin and lignin. The compost made from saw dust and sewage sludge is found highly suitable for growing button mushroom which is prepared in combination with nitrogen, phosphate and potash fertilizers. They will be used in the definite proportions. Otherwise the production will be less. Different ingredients can be used but the requisite proportion must be maintained for a good production. The ratio of carbohydrate to nitrogen (C. N.) should be 17:1. Carbohydrate-rich substances are grass, straw, leaves and twigs, seed, bark etc. Wheat bran too contains plenty of carbohydrates. It is needless to say that the importance of nitrogen is also vital, If nitrogen is deficient in the compost the rate of production will be less. The percentage of nitrogen in the compost should be 3 just at the time of spawning. In the first phase of making compost much of nitrogen changes into ammonia gas. In the later stage that ammonia is mixed with the microbial protein to from a product which is very useful food for mushroom. It should borne in mind that nitrogen obtained from organic residues is more useful than that from the chemical sources. Because organic nitrogen exists with carbon, potassium and phosphorus. Besides in the process of decomposition of organic substance heat is generated which is very favourable for the growth of mycenium. As a source of organic nitrogen poultry manure can be used. In poultry manure the ratio of carbohydrate to nitrogen is nearly 17:1 which is considered useful for button mushroom. If poultry manure is used less in the compost nitrogen should be supplemented by the use of urea or ammonium nitrate.

TECHNIQUE

The processes of composting, e.g. long and short methods are in practice. For the first method 3-4 week time is required and for the second only a period of 12 days is sufficient.

LONG METHOD

Compost will be prepared on a clean cemented floor under a shed with its four sides open. If it is to be made in the open a sheet of polythene is required to protect the compost from the sun and shower. In case a room is used the ventilation must be good.

On the basis of the ingredients used the compost has been classified into two types which are discussed below.

NATURAL COMPOST

It is prepared from horse dung. In the stable plenty of straw is used as litter for the horses. Dung, litter, urine are mixed together to from stable manure. If litter is not used in the stable straw should necessarily be mixed with dung and urine. The quantity of straw (in weight) should be one-thirds of the dung used. The compost pile must not be exposed to the sun and shower. After 3-4 days the fermentation will start and consequently the temperature within the pile will increase and ammonia gas will evolve. To effect aeration the pile should be broken and be piled again as before. The process will be repeated

4-5 times at an interval of 4-5 days. Towards the last operations some gypsum has to be mixed at the rate of 25 kg. per tonne of compost.

SYNTHETIC COMPOST

The following ingredients are required for composting.

Wheat or paddy straw (8-10 cm cuttings) .... 25 kg.

Wheat bran .... 25 kg.

Ammonium sulphate/Cal. Ammo. Nitrate .... 400 g.

Urea .... 30 g.

Gypsum .... 2 kg.

Soak the straw cuttings in water on a clean cemented floor. Mix other ingredients excepting wheat bran with the soaked straw thoroughly. Then pile the mixture. The shape of the pile should be rectangular. The width and height of the pile should be one metre each. The length depends on the quantity of the compost materials.

1 Wheat straw (30 cm cuttings) .... 100 kg.
Paddy straw (30 cm. cuttings) .... 100 kg.
Cal. Amm. Nitrate .... 3 kg.
Super phosphate .... 3 kg.
Urea .... 1 kg.
Wheat bran .... 10 kg.
Gypsum .... 4 kg.
Chalk dust ($CaCO_3$) .... 3 kg.

The straw should be soaked for 48 hours, then other ingredients should be mixed with it.

2 Horse manure .... 200 kg.
Wheat straw .... 100 kg.
Poultry manure .... 50 kg.
Wheat bran .... 15 kg.
Urea .... 3 kg.
Gypsum .... 10 kg.

3 Paddy straw .... 33 kg.
Poultry manure .... 10 kg.
Wheat bran .... 1.5 kg.
Gypsum .... 1 kg.

4 (Innovated by Seth in 1975)

Wheat straw	1 tonne
Cal.amm. nitrate	30 kg.
Super phosphate	25 kg.
Urea	12 kg.
Sulphate of potash	100 kg.
Wheat bran	16.5 lt.
Thin mollasses	100 kg.
Nemagon (Nematocide)	266 ml.

Schedule for turning the pile

Ist day	Piling
Ist turning	On the fifth day (the half each of urea and CAN should be added).
2nd turning	On the 7th day (molasses to be added).
3rd turning	On the 10th day (gypsum and Nemagon to be added. Then fill the trays with compost).

The compost used in Taiwan

Paddy straw	100 kg.
Urea	1 kg.
Ammonium sulphate	2 kg.
Super phosphate	2 kg.
Chalk dust	2 kg.
Lime (Air-slaked, CaOH)	2 kg.
Water	200 lt.

PROCESS OF COMPOSITING

Soak straw cuttings in the solution of lime and pile the material for two days. Then mix other ingredients and the required quantity of water and pile again as before. On the 4th day break the pile for aeration and pile again on a sheet of polythene spread on the cemented floor. Prick the pile at several points with a pointed stick so that the materials lying in the centre get aerated. If 2-3 perforated plastic tubes are placed inside the pile and their ends remain in the outside the aeration will take place easily. Cover the pile with a sheet of polythene. The tube ends should remain outside the polythene cover. Adopting this technique compost can be prepared within 10-12 days.

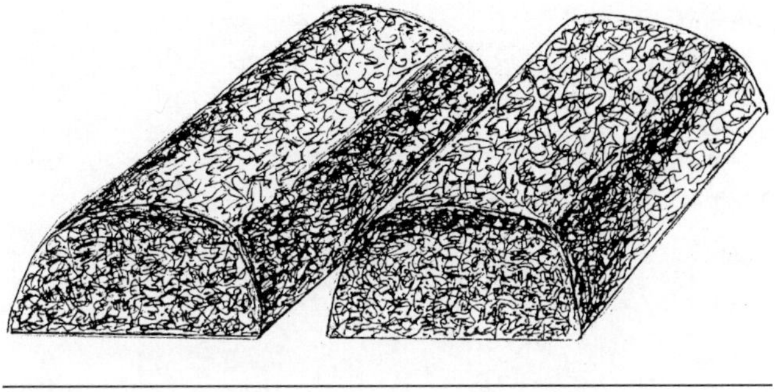

Fig. 7: Heaps of compost.

SPAWN AND SPAWNING

Mycelium is known as mushroom seed. It is grown in a bottle under a controlled condition of a laboratory. Seed bottles are sold to or distributed among the farmers. Obviously the seed is of a particular species and the seed bottle is labeled with the name of that species. Mycelium is known as *mushroom spawn.*

Fill the trays with compost almost up to the rim. Break the bottle to release the spawn. Scatter the grain spawn over the surface of compost and work into a depth of 5-7 cm. firming the compost afterwards.

If the quality of seed is high the production can be optimum. The seed must be of a particular species but never should be mixed. Therefore a scientific purity is a must.

The mushroom culture was started in the 17th century. Then compost was prepared from the dung of a stable. The compost beds were spawned with the mycelium collected from the mushroom beds after harvest. Since then the mycelium is known as spawn.

DIFFERENT TYPES OF SPAWN

1. **Vergin Spawn :** Mycelium is produced by sowing spores of a particular species on the suitable substrate. If mycelium is grown thick with the inter woven hyphae a lump with some substrate can be used for spawning. This type of spawn is known as 'Virgin spawn'. Atkinson writes in 1962 that France would export vergin spawn to other countries.

2. **Flake Spawn :** When the compost of a bed is covered with the mycelium growth just before raising pin heads break the compost bed and dry the mycelium. The dry compost flakes with mycelium can be used to spawn the new compost beds.

3. **Brick Spawn :** Cast a layer of 3 cm. thickness with a mixture of the following materials.

   - Horse dung
   - Cow dung
   - Loam
   - Water

   Then cut it into small brick-like pieces. A small depression on each brick is made and mycelium is put into the depressions. For few days keep the bricks in a moist condition. This will favour the growth of mycelium which will cover the brick. These mycelium - covered bricks can be used for spawning.

4. **Grain Spawn :** In this process grains are used as a medium for growing mycelium. Wheat or rye is used for this purpose. Grain spawn is very popular and used widely by the farmers of all levels. On making spawn the grain used may be clotted. To prevent it Stoler has recommended in 1962 to mix 6 g of gypsum and 1.5 g of chalk dust with one pound (450 g) of grain. Kumar and his associates say (1975) that it will be better if boiled millet is used instead of wheat. Two per cent gypsum and 6 per cent pulverized chalk should be mixed with the grain. The process is very suitable for producing spawn of buttom mushroom.

In 1972, Tiwan scientist Hu and with a view to producing granular spawn they used pulverized oyester shells ($CaCO_3$), starch, powdered compost and wheat bran. They succeeded in producing a good compost by this methods.

SPAWING

The quality of mushroom to be produced is dependant on the quantity of spawn used. The spawning technique will be discussed here.

1. **Double-layer spawning**: The tray is half - filled with compost. The spawn blocks are placed on the compost at a uniform spacing. Then the tray is completely filled with compost, at the top the spawn blocks are placed as before. They are pressed into the compost with the finger tips. On spawning cover the trays with a polythene sheet.

2. **Top spawning**: The tray is filled with compost. After spawning a light dressing of compost is applied.

3. **Through spawning**: Compost is mixed with the spawn grains thoroughly and then the tray is filled with it.

4. **Shake-up spawning**: The usefulness of this technique has been proved to be better by many researchers. A week after spawning the compost is taken out and stirred to disturb. Then the trays are again filled with it. The next operation is casing, i.e. covering the compost with a thin layer of paste-like puddled mud.

5. **Active mycelium spawning**: It was innovated in Germany. Just before raising pin heads the mycelium covers the compost of the trays. In this stage the compost mass of one tray is disturbed and the mycelium is used for spawning other trays just filled with compost.

6. **Spot spawning**: Small holes are made on the compost with the finger tips. Spawn is placed into the holes which are then filled with compost and pressed with the finger tips.

7. **Super spawning**: The trays are filled with pasteurized compost which is spawned as usual. After two weeks the compost of all trays are taken out. All the compost are taken together and stirred to disturb. A fresh lot of compost of the same volume is mixed with it. This mixture is used to fill the trays which will obviously be the double of the first lot.

The utility of these methods in our climates has been tested by Sandilya and his associates in 1974. In their experiments, they have found that the thorough spawning and double-layer spawning are better than any other methods in our conditions.

CASING

After spawning the surface of the compost is covered with a layer of puddled clay. This operation is known as 'casing' which is a must in the cultural operations. The reasons are discussed below.

1. Without casing the weight of a fruit body will be less.

2. Casing can preserve moisture of the compost for a long time, which is indispensable for growing quality products in good quantities.

3. The fruit bodies sprout from mycelium when it faces the shortage of nutrition after its growth in the different medium. Casing favours to bring about this condition early.

4. The temperature of the bed of compost is controlled to some extent by casing. The best ingredients for making the puddle for casing have been recommended by Atkin in 1972.
   i) A good casing can absorb water readily and pass it slowly to the compost underneath.
   ii) It should be porous to favour aeration.
   iii) The texture of the casing material should remain unchanged when soaked in water.
   iv) The puddle for casing should be neutral i.e. not acid, nor alkaline (pH 7).
   v) It should be free form pests and the germs of diseases. The organic matter yet to decompose must not be in the puddle.
   vi) The French farmers first unerstood the utility of casing and it was proved in case of button mushroom. Casing helps change the active vegetative phase into the reproductive phase, i.e. the stage of sprouting fruit bodies that bears spores to complete the life cycle.
5. The exposed mycelium on the compost are prone to form stroma which does not favour the formation of fruit bodies. Therefore casing is indispensable.

All these prove that the casing is a must for growing button mushroom which has been accepted by the farmers all over the world.

In the early stage pulverised lime stone ($CaCO_3$) was used in France. In the later stage common soil was considered the best material for casing. In 1070 Lust found that the best material for casing is the mixture of loam, cow manure and leaf mould. Some ingredients are recommended for this purpose in this country. They are i)good manure and sandy soil at the ratio of 3:1; ii) clay and sand (1:1); iii) Farmyard manure and grit (4:1); iv) Farmyard manure and loam (1:1); v) Compost, sand and slaked lime (4:1:1). Lambert and Hamfeld have said in 1039 that casing materials must be neutral (pH 7). They have found by experiments that acid or alkaline reaction does not favour a good production.

A simple casing compost has been innovated by the author. Mix fine-textured sandy loam with pure leaf mould (1:1). Before mixing the leaf mould should be seived through 2mm. mesh. Soak the compost in the formalin solution (2%) and kept covered for 48 hours. Then keep it open for escaping the formalin gas for a week. Before casing add water to make a paddle of pliable consistency.

PASTEURIZATION

If the material is pasteurized the production will be high. By applying heat or chemical sterilants the soil can be made germ-free. Steam generated in a boiler is passed through the perforated tubes which are laid in the soil to be sterilized. If the soil is subjected to a temperature of 60 °C for five hours the germs will be killed. It should be borne in mind that high-pressure steam cannot be applied as it kills the useful microbes of the soil.

Fig. 8: Mushroom bed made on the floor of a room.

As the chemical sterilants formalin, chloropicrin, mythael bromide, vapam etc. are used. Of them formalin is very popular and widely used. 500ml. of formalin is mixed with 10 litres of water for treating 1 cubic meter of soil to be used for casing. Spread the soil in a thin layer on a sheet of polythene. Spray the formalin solution on it. Then pile the treated soil and cover it with a polythene sheet for 48 hours. After a week the formalin gas will escape from the soil and then it can be used for casing.

When casing should be done is not yet certain; because the workers hold the different views. Some are of the opinion that the casing should be done immediately after spawning; but others say that it will be better if it is done several days after spawning. It is however accepted on all hands that one should not do anything risky. If the compost remains opens it is likely to be infected by diseases. Besides there is a harmful fly that lay eggs on the open compost. That fly is known as 'mushroom fly'.

The thickness of casing should necessarily be uniform. Because water on sprinkling should moisten the compost below the casing uniformly. Besides the pin heads can pierce the thin layer of casing. The thickness of casing should be 2.5-4 cm.

PICKING FRUIT BODIES

Generally from 15-20 days after casing the fruit bodies begin to rise. At times water should be sprinkled. For this purpose sprayer or sprinkler should be used. The humidity of the room should be 70-80 per cent, or the compost of the trays will tend to dry resulting in the bad growth of mycelium. The ventilation within the room should be normal or the quantity of carbon dioxide will increase, which will cause harm to the crop. If heat and humidity be increased the incidence of the pests and diseases will occur. For this reason the temperature should be at 14-16 °C. No bad smell should be there in the room. If the ventilation is good no foul smell can be experienced. In the dry weather the soil of casing will run dry. To prevent this condition damp the floor by sprikling water.

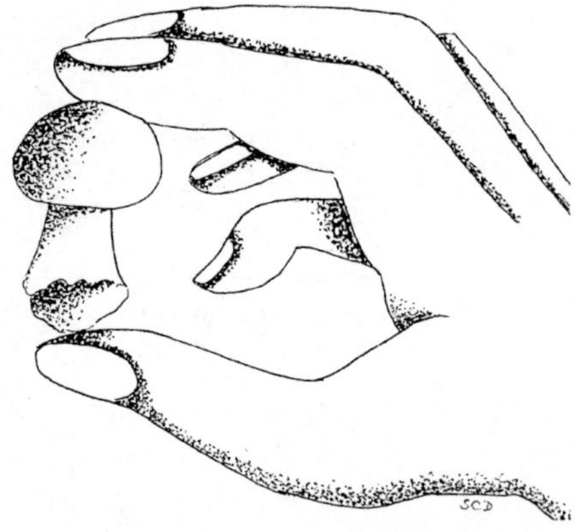

Fig. 9: A button mushroom between two fingers.

The fruit bodies rise collectively, i.e. in flocks and in successive batches. Fruit bodies are formed in the temperature of 15 °C. It takes a week to attain the size of a large button. The time gap between the first and the second batch is usually 10 days. After a few batches the mushroom will comparatively be small.

When the mushrooms should be picked ?. It is a pertinent question, of course. When the veil will be loose and remain free from the cap the mushroom becomes ready for picking. Still the cap remain tight. When the cap becomes loose the gill turn brown indicating the formation of spores has started.

Mushroom are picked up by twisting the stem gently off the soil. The base of the stalk with the soil clinging to it is clipped off.

Mushroom should be picked in the early hours of the day by light twisting so that the broken stump (stub) is not left over in the trays and the small enveloping mushrooms are not disturbed. Those will be picked when the diameter of the cap is less than 3 cm. for selling to the canning unit. For fresh sale even the bigger sized can be harvested preferably before the rapture of the veil.

The stalk must be cut at the soil line and packed neatly in 250 or 500g packings in the perforated polythene bags or in paper bags. In the sophisticated markets of the cities especially in the new market (Lindsay street) of Calcutta. They are sold by the green grocers.

If a small pin head grows very close to a large fruit body cut the stalk of the large mushroom with a sharp knife so that the small pin head is not disturbed. Because it is yet to grow. The cavities formed due to picking of mushrooms should be filled with some compost which is pressed with fingers. After picking the room should be cleaned and mushroom can be picked for 6-7 weeks but in the shelf system, for 6-12 weeks.

DISEASE CONTROL

If the compost, casing material and the room for keeping tryas are made germ-free the incidence of diseases will not take place. The excess humidity, temperature and poor ventilation are likely to cause the disease infection. The clean and tidy environment helps keep disease at day.

1. **Cobweb Mildew :** On the casing of the bed a mould resembling a thin layer of wet cotton is found to grow. The colour is white which turns pink in the later stage. This fungus growth attacks mushroom. The affected fruit bodies look like a puffy cotton ball. But the inside of the ball is rotten. In the excessive humid condition and poor ventilation this mould occurs. As a remedy Dithane M-48 (0.2%) can be sprayed.

Secondly before placing the trays the room should be sprayed with formalin.

2. **Brown Plaster Mould :** On spawning a white mould may be seen. It turns brown afterwards. This mould spread very rapidly and affect the rate of production. The compost is already infected with the spores of this mould. But it starts growing when the humidity and the temperature of the room increase considerably. In excessive humidity and high temperature (28-32 °C) this mould do much harm to the crop. It is checked by spraying 2 per cent formalin.

3. **Olive-Green Mould :** This mould appears just after spawning and before casing. The colour of the mould is white which turns olive green afterwards. If the compost is not well pulverized poor ventilation and the excessive moisture of the compost are the causes of the disease. The affected parts should be sprayed with 2 per cent Captan or 0.05 per cent Benlate to control this disease.

4. **Green Mould :** On the casing a green mould may appear. This mould affects the formation of fruit bodies. The spores of this fungus are carried by wind and water. Spray 0.05 per cent of Benlate to control the disease.

5. **Truffle Disease :** It appears in summer. In appearance it looks like very small-sized mushroom. The colour is cream, the shape is round, coiled or crinkled. Its wrinkled top looks like the brain. In the last stage it turns brown and busts to eject spores. Excessive humidity and poor ventilation are the causes of the disease. The room temperature below 18 °C and the normal ventiation do not help develop this mould. The humidity of the room need not be high.

6. **Bubble Disease :** On the top of the mushroom fungus grows in a twisted form. The production of the affected bed is lowered. The cap of the infected mushroom becomes small and the stalk grows thicker than usual.

   Generally infection comes from the infected materials of casing. If the temperature of the beds rises above 17 °C this disease infection takes place. The infected fruit bodies should be sprayed with formalin. Then they will be picked and burnt. After this the beds should be sprayed with 0.2 per cent of Dithane M-45 and 0,05 per cent Benlate one after another.

7. **Dry Bubble Disease :** Due to this disease brown spots appear on the top of the cap. Generally they grow larger and merge with each other. The heavily affected cap assumes a twisted shape.

   Generally the infection spreads from the casing materials. The high temperature and poor ventilation are favourable for the incidence of this disease. To prevent the infection the beds should be applied at the time of casing and the second when the pin heads are seen and the last after the picking of the mushroom of the second batch.

ECONOMICS OF INPUTES AND OUTPUTS

The commercial culture of button mushroom is profitable. Even one can make profits by growing in the cottage scale. Moreover the profits come within a very short time. A compost of 100 kg. of straw yield 40 kg of mushroom. In the retail markets button mushroom are sold at Rs. 100.00 per kg. The wholesale price being Rs. 50-60.00 per kg. The price of 40 kg. is 2000.00 (Rs. 50.00 per kg). Button mushroom is costlier than any other cultivated mushrooms. Hence the profit is high. The cost of growing is Rs. 20-25.00 per kg. of mushroom. Therefore the net profit will be nearly Rs. 1000.00 to Rs. 1200.00. Besides it has a by-product. After picking the last batch of the crop the compost is treated as a good manure for other agricultural purposes.

Cultivation of Oyester Mushroom

Many species of oyester mushroom are found in India. One species is found to be grown on the dead branches and logs. It is more fleshy, usually not eaten though edible.

One species named *Pleurotus sajor-caju* is cultivated widely in this country. Its culture is easier than that of white button mushroom. The rate of production is also higher. The fruit bodies are very beautiful. Hence attractive. The nutritive value is also good but the taste is not so delicious as that of white button mushroom (*A. bisporus*) and paddy-straw mushroom (*Volvariella* spp.). For this reason oyester mushroom is less popular. Though it is easy to grow and nutritive too, many people add other protein-rich food articles to it to make most delicious recipes.

Food value of oyester mushroom (*P. sajor caju*). Findings of Jandaik and Kapur, 1975 on dry weight basis.

Ascorbic acid 0.06%
Fat 2.26%
Protein 47.93%
Sugar 0.285%
Starch.. 0.120%

CULTURAL METHODS

Although the basic principles are the same with some modifications a number of processes have been innovated. *Pleurotus sajor-caju* is known as *Dhingri* in Hindi.

METHOD No. 1

Dhingri is grown well on shelves or on rope cost. Dhingri grown on a rope cot (2m × 1m) has been illustrated in this book. The day temperature of 20-30 °C is highly suitable for growing oyester mushroom. The ingredients required for making compost are given below.

Straw (chips of 1-2.5 cm) .... 15 kg (dry weight)
Suphala 15:15:15 .... 3 kg.

Or

Straw (chips 1-2.5 cm long .... 15 kg
Urea .... 325 g.
Super phosphate .... 800 g.
Sulphate of potash/Muriate of potash .... 300-600 g.

Soak the straw chips in water for 24 hours. The excess water is drained off. Keep two-fifths of the soaked straw apart. The rest (3/5) is mixed with fertilizer mix thoroughly.

On the cot spread a piece of nylon mosquito netting. over it spread the straw mixed with fertilizer in the uniform thickness. Then over it spread 1/10 of the straw chips without fertilizer. Scatter the spawn of 2 bottles over this layer. Then cover the spawn with a layer of the same quantity of straw chips. Over this layer scatter the spawn of 2 bottles uniformly. Cover the spawn with a layer of the rest of the straw chips.

Cover the pile of compost with the two fold hessian cloth. In case of the shortage of moisture in the pile remove the hessian cover ad spray water as required. Replace the cover immediately.

Nearly after 25 days of spawning pin heads appear. Remove the cover of hessian cloth. After 3-4 days the fruit bodies will come up. The next batch of the crop can be picked after 10 days of picking the first batch. From a pile of 30 kg straw on a cot 20 kg of mushroom can be obtained. After each batch of picking the pile will be covered and sprinkled with water to maintain the desired level of moisture.

Fig. 10: Shelves of nylon cord netting for bed of oyester mushroom.

METHOD No. 2

A new technique of mushroom cultivation has been innovated, which is simple, easy to adopt and cheep. By this method the housewives who grow vegetable in the kitchen garden will be able to grow mushroom in a small nylon bag.

Straw (1 kg) is chopped to the bits of 1-2.5 cm long. Soak the straw chips in water for 24 hours. Drain off the excess water. Two fifths of the spawn is kept apart which will be used for covering the spawn. The fertilizer-mix will be mixed with the remaining 3/5 parts of straw. As a fertilizer 200 grams of N-P-K- 15:15:15 is enough. Therefore, 200 grams of *Suphala* 15:15:15 can be used for the purpose. The following ingredients can be used as the substitute.

Urea .... 66 g.

Super phosphate .... 166 g.

Sulphate of potash/muriate of potash .... 60 g.

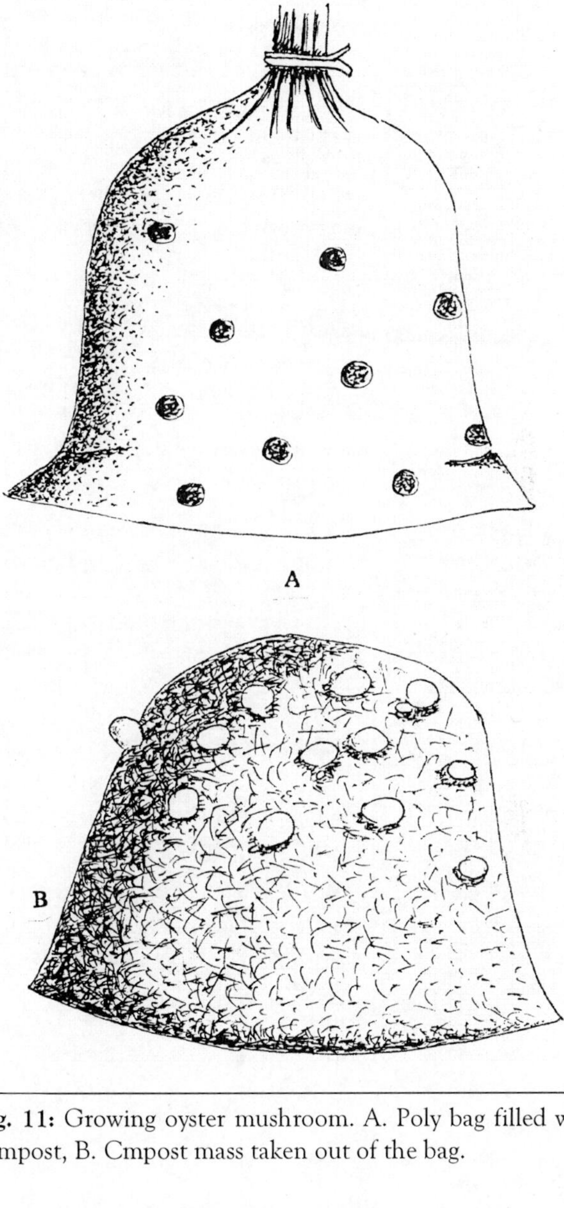

A

B

Fig. 11: Growing oyster mushroom. A. Poly bag filled with compost, B. Cmpost mass taken out of the bag.

Fill a bag of nylon netting (45cm × 30cm) with the straw mixed with fertilizer. Over it spread 1/10 of the straw (already set apart for this purpose) to from a layer. Over this layer scatter 1/4 spawn of a bottle. Cover the spawn with a layer of straw as before. Over it scatter 1/4 spawn of a bottle which is covered as before with a layer of the straw. Then the net bag has to be put in a plastic bag with a number of holes punched on either side. Close the mouth of the bag by tying with a cord. Hang it with a rope from the ceiling of the shed or verandah. At an interval of few days open the plastic bag to check if watering is needed. On watering the mouth of the bag will be closed again.

Nearly after three weeks the pin heads will appear when the plastic bag should be removed. The remaining operations are the same as the method no.1. From a bag 500-800 g of mushroom can be obtained.

METHOD No.3

Bano and his associates have developed a simple method of growing *Pleurotus flabellatus* in 1974, which is described below.

Straw (1 kg) is chopped to the bits of 1-2 cm long. Soak it in hot water (60-70 °C) for 10-15 minutes. In the morning drain off the water. For a kilo of straw (dry weight) 8 g of four of horse gram (*Dolichos biflorus*) and 20 g of grain spawn are required. The flour of any other pulse can also be used instead. These two ingredients (pulse flour and spawn) are mixed with the soaked straw. A plastic bag is filled with the fertilizer-straw mix. A number of holes were punched on either side of the bag. Keep the bag in a room temperature of 21-35 °C. When the pin heads will appear the temperature should be lowered to 25-28 °C. This temperature is very conducive to growing more pin heads. When the pin heads are found to appear the lump of straw should be taken out by tearing away the bag.

To raise the moisture content watering may be needed more than once a day. Within a few days from all parts of the surface of the lump the fruit bodies will be growing.

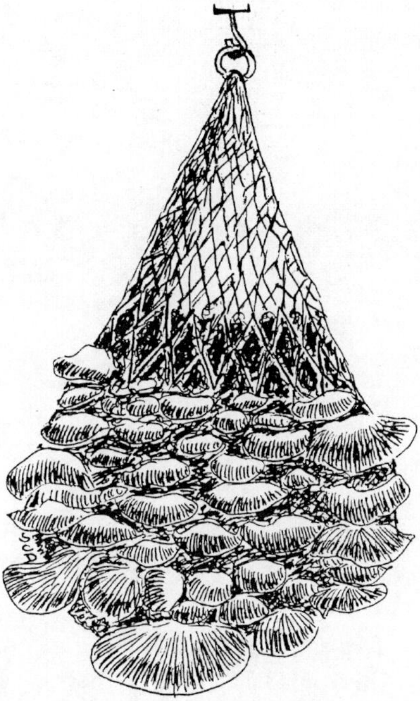

Fig. 13: Oyster mushroom grown in a bag of nylon netting.

Growing Paddy-Straw Mushroom

In Bengali it is called *Poal Chhatu,* because most of the mushrooms are umbrella-like. Hence the name *Chhatu*. It is derived from *Chhata*, the umbrella. Paddy straw is termed *Poal* in Bengali.

Paddy straw is exclusively needed for growing *Volvariella* species. They cannot be grown in the straws of other cereals. In the coastal region the continuous heavy rains decompose the paddy straw in the farmyard. *Volvariella volvacea* is found to grow on decomposed straw from June--October when the day temperature varies from 30 °C to 35 °C. Even in the concave joints a paddy-straw thatch where the straw decomposes fast *Volvariella* grows there in August to September. Now-a-days it is grown with the help of the grain spawn and paddy straw commercially. It is known that *Volvariella* was grown in China in the eighteenth century. There it is known as 'Chinese mushroom' 'Tributary mushroom' or 'Nauhua mushroom'. In China and in those parts of South-east Asia where the Chinese population is considerable paddy-straw mushroom is in great demand. They regard it as one of the delicious and nutritious foods, and as such it is sold at a high price. It is legendary that in the Nauhua temple of China it was first grown by the Buddhist monks. They were vegetarian, as such, fond of mushroom. In the rice growing area of this country on the heaps of straw waste in the farmyard *Volvariella* grows in quantities which are consumed by the farmers as a delicious food article. In the eastern part of the country the village people with a view to getting more mushroom scatter *beson* (flour of pulse) on the stack of paddy straw in the beginning of mushroom. Without spawning a good quantity of mushroom is obtained in this method.

In this country the scientific culture of *Volvariella* was first experimentally started at Coimbatore. It requires high temperature more than any other cultivated mushroom. The congenial temperature for its ideal growth being 30-35 °C. Therefore in the plains it can be grown from March to October. Besides paddy straw other ingredients like cotton waste and water hyacinth (*Eichhornia crassipes*) can also be used. Of the genus *Volvariella* three species namely *V. diplasia*, *V. volvacea* and *V. esculenta* are grown in this country. The cultural methods are described below.

The leafy top of the bundle of straw is removed. Soak the bundle in water for 24 hours. To soak completely they are immersed in the water contained in a cistern. To facilitate it some weights like bricks, blocks, stones logs etc. are put on them. After taking out of the pool of water keep it for an hour to drain off the excess water. Then on a bamboo frame the bundles are stacked in layers. The frame is held 30 cm above the floor by a number of supports of bricks. Now-a-days the farmers use the rope cots for this purpose. To prevent rotting the nylon ropes are used instead of the just twines. The straw stack of several layers should be equal in length and breadth. The heads of the bundles of a layer must be in one direction. In the next layer all the heads of the bundles should be in the opposite direction. By this process of arrangement the height would be the same in all parts of the stack. For spawning these two layers of straw bundles will from a composite layer. Scatter the grain spawn towards the border of the stack. Sprinkle some *besan* on the spawn. Then repeat the process as before i.e. spawning above the two layers of straw bundles. The heads of these two layers (3rd & 4th would be at right angle to the first and second layers. The fifth and sixth layer will be arranged just as the first and the second layers. Above the sixth layer spawning should be repeated as before. in each time over the spawn *besan* should be sprinkled.

Above the six layer after spawning the spawn should be covered with a layer of wet straw. Then press the stack to make it compact. The stack of this size needs grain spawn of 350-400g.

To increase the size of the fruit bodies chemical fertilizer should be applied. For this purpose a mixture of ammonium sulphate (560g) and super phosphate (112g) should be applied in three equal parts on the three layers of spawning. Apply it by scattering after spawning. This extra nutrients help produce more mycelium than usual. The last operation being to cover the stack with a sheet of polythene. The temperature inside the stack should rise to 30-35 °C. At the temperature below 30 °C the pin heads will not appear. The pin heads will grow within 7-10 days of spawning. It will take few days more to have the full size of a mushroom. The correct time of picking is the condition when the cap will start splitting at the periphery. The pin head will appear in three batches at an interval of 10 days.

Fig. 14: Paddy straw mushroom grown on a stack of paddy straw.

Thomas and his associates have developed a new method of growing *V. esculenta* in 1943. For this purpose make a platform of 75 cm × 75 cm of wooden planks at a height of 30 cm. A straw rope of 21 m long and 7 cm diameter is made by spinning. For making three layers three pieces of straw ropes 21 m each should be made.

Soak the ropes in a cistern of water for 24 hours. For the first layer one rope is laid in the zigzag way as illustrated. Sow the seed (spawn) on this layer. In each layer spawning should be made in the same way as in the foregoing method. At the end after watering exact pressure to make the stack compact. Then cover the stack with a sheet of polythene as usual.

Fig. 15: Mushroom bed on paddy straw spinned to from a rope.

POLY-BAG METHOD

Straw chips are soaked in water for 24 hours. Soak some news paper (1/4 of the straw) in water for few hours. Straw, paper pulp and spawn are mixed together and a polythene bag is filled with the mix. The bag must have some holes punched on either side to effect aeration. The bag should be placed where the temperature remains from 35-40 °C. After a week tear away the bag and take out the lump. Place it on the wood plank. In a dry weather keep it moist by sprinkling water over it.

Paddy-straw mushroom needs more moisture than any other mushroom. Therefore the relative humidity of the surroundings should be 80--90 per cent. The pin heads will begin to appear ten days after filling the bag with the mix.

Alicbusan has developed another simple method which is suitable for the village people in 1979. In this method straw will be soaked for three hours only. Then it is heaped on a bamboo frame lined with a polythene sheet. Take four litres of water in a plastic bucket. Mix only 3 g of urea with it. Then mix with it some newspaper cut into small pieces. The quantity of paper should be such as to soak the water of the bucket. Spawn is mixed with the paper pulp. A pinch of the mix is added to the soaked straw heap by putting 5 cm apart in a depth of 4 cm by a finger tip. Water need to be sprinkled to attain the desired moisture level. The pin head will begin to appear in a week or so. Alicbusan was of the opinion that a little soil should be mixed with the straw to make a better substrate. This bed can be made in a shed or under the shede of a tree. To grow outdoors a polythene sheet is needed to protect the heap from the rains.

PEST AND DISEASE CONTROL

I f the bed is infected with fungus the production will be reduced. The common mould are *Aspergillus* spp., *Rhizaphus stonelifera rolfsii*. Besides *Coprinus artatus* and *Sathyrella* spp. are found to grow in special cases. The moulds are controlled by spraying fungicides. Captan and Zineb are very effective to destroy moulds. It is interesting to note that these two fungicides kill other fungi only but do not harm mushroom though it is a fungus. Mites, snails and slugs cause harm to mushroom. To remove mites spray Malathion and to control snails and slugs scatter *Mahua* oilcake in the powdered from around the mushroom beds. It can also be sprinkled over the bed. Malathion (0.025%) and Benlate (0.025%) are mixed together to spray the beds. It will destroy the pests and disease causing fungi.

SHAPE AND SIZE OF THE BED

The production of mushroom depends to a great extent on the shape and size of the bed. The heap or stack of straw which is termed as 'substrate' is called 'bed' for growing mushroom. The small beds tends to dry quickly, where as the large bed in the centre of which the temperature rises to exceed the optimum level is also bad in this respect.

The recommendations of some research workers in this regard are laid down below.

Krishnamurthi and Latika Kumari has recommended (1966) that the size of the bed should be 1m x 1m. But according to Gupta and his associate it should be 1/2m × 1/2m × 60.

Favourable temperature

For growing *Volvariella* the temperature should not go below 30 °C.

PRESERVATION

It is very difficult to preserve paddy-straw mushroom. Therefore it is better to consume fresh by cooking. But on drying and then cooking they can be canned to preserve. The mushroom grown in shade can be preserved four hours more than those grown in the full sun. It was proved by an experiment by Kaul in 1978. According to him the paddy straw-mushroom can be grown in a light intensity of 4-18 lux. The fresh *Volvariella* can be preserved in refrigerator (10-15 °C) for 48 hours. If immersed in 10% brine for few minutes the mushroom, thus treated, can be preserved for 7 days. *Volavariella* contains 78 per cent of water. Therefore, on drying their weight is reduced to 22%. In other words, 1 kg. of *Volvariella* on drying will give weigh 220 g only. For dehydration of *Volvariella* temperature of 55-60 °C is needed. Dry mushroom can absorb moisture readily from the moist air. Therefore, thoroughly dried mushroom can be preserved in a hermetically sealed pouches of aluminium foil. If not thoroughly dried it will emit a foul smell white cooking.

METHOD OF CANNING

Just before opening of the pin heads *Volvariella* should be picked. For preserving in a tin after cooking cut into small pieces, wash them thoroughly in water. Then put them in boiling water for 3-4 minutes. On cooling immerse them in 2% brine in a tin and seal it air tight. Then for pasteurization put the sealed tin in a steam of 10 lb pressure for 40 minutes. After this process keep the tins in a cool place.

Now-a-days *Volvariella* is sold in the village bazaars in the rains. They are collected from the rotton straw heaps of the farmyard. There are also a number of other mushroom collected from the semi-forest or fallow lands. Of all these *Volvariella* has a great demand and sold at the highest price, say at rupees fifty to eighty per kilo gram.

Preparing Grain Spawn

The mushroom spawn which is artificially prepared in the laboratory is the sterile mycelium. The spores grow on the gills. They are very minute. From one pelius a few million spores are produced. Those spores on humus or compost germinate to from a hypha. The hypha grows to from a net-like structure which is known as mycelium. The pin heads grow from the mycelium, which within a few days develop into the umbrella-like mushroom. The spores are very minute, nearly microscopic. How they will be collected is discussed below.

Remove the stalk (stipe) from the cap (pelius) by a sharp knife. Place the cap on a white paper so that the gills just touch the paper or remain very close to the paper. Cover the cap with a bell jar or with an inverted plastic pot. After 4-6 hours remove the cap from the paper which will be like a printed paper. The minute spores have stuck to the paper, which cannot be rubbed off easily. Hence called 'paper print'. This however, has to be done early in the morning within an hour of opening the cap. The dried spores can be preserved in a glass bottle. If they are sown on compost will germinate to form hyphae in the moist condition. The compost with the mycelium growth can be used as spawn.

When grain (Cereal) is used to make spawn such spawn is known as 'grain spawn' Wheat or millet is used to grow spawn. The grain will be free from impurities and insect infestation. The grain partly eaten up by insects must be removed. The grain already treated with fungicide or insecticide should not be used.

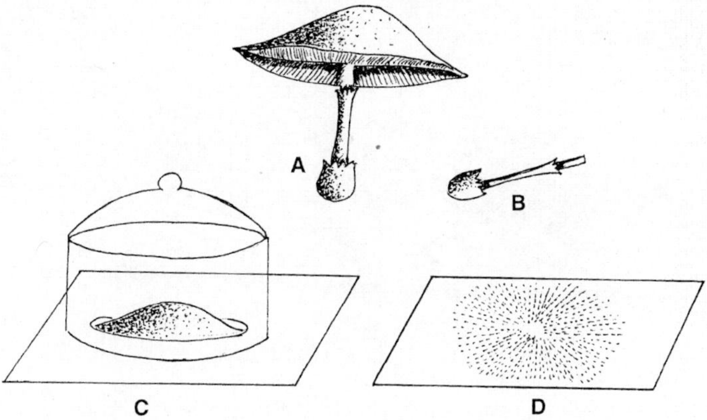

Fig. 16: Collection of spores by paper print process. A. A whole mushroom, B. Stipe without cap, C. Cap on a paper under a bell jar, D. Cap is removed, spores are found to stick to the paper

The grain will be boiled with the half of its volume of water. It should not over boiled to from starch. The grain will burst when starch will be formed. If some quantity of water still remain it should be drained off. Spread the grain on a sheet of polythene for sometime. Then mix chalk dust with the grain at a ratio of 1:8 (chalk : grain). Then fill a bottle with the grain and close the lid. Pasteurize the bottle in a autoclave with a steam of 15 lb (Psi) pressure for half an hour a day in two installments. The chalk dust will absorb excess water from the grain thereby preventing the lump formation. Besides it will increase the pH; i.e. acidity will be removed. After two days take out the bottles from the autoclave and add the spawn cultured in the incubator to the grain of the bottles. The bottles will be kept in a temperature from 24-26 °C for three weeks. By this time the grain will be covered with the mycelium. This method is adopted to grow the spawn of *Agaricus bisporus*. It is also applicable to growing the spawn of *Volvariella* spp. and *Pleurotus* spp. In case of *Volvariella* paddy-straw chips (4-6 cm long) instead of grain can be used. Soak the straw chips in water overnight. Next morning drain off the excess of water. Mix *besan* of gram with the straw chips at the ratio of 1:8 (by weight of soaked straw). Fill the 3/4 parts of the bottle with the mix. Then the spawn culture of *Volvareilla* has to be added to the content of the bottle. Keep it for 10 days at the temperature 30-38 °C. Within 15 days the straw chips will be covered with the mycelium and clamidospore of bright colour will be found to grow. It looks like a gland.

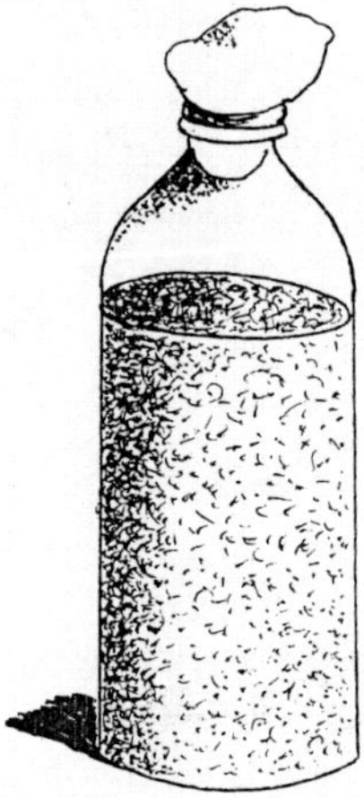

Fig. 17: Grain spawn grown in a bottle.

PREPARING CULTURE

The culture is prepared from a part of the mushroom body or its spore. It is better to have a part adjacent to the cap and stipe for this purpose. It should be borne in mind that the mother culture does not remain intact for a long time. But it can be preserved in a temperature near 4 °C in a refrigerator. If the mother culture is propagated in other pots successively the deficiency of food in the culture medium does not occur. A culture is lost when the food deficiency occurs in the medium. For propagation a sterilized pipet must be used.

Do's and Dont's of Mushroom Growing

1. Make copost with care. At the time of spawing the compost should not emit the foul smell which is of ammonia.
2. At the time of filling the trays the compost should not be too wet.
3. A good compost is a key to success. Therefore make a good compost.
4. The trays should be filled to the rim with compost.
5. Collect the spawn from a reliable firm.
6. The contaminated seeds should not be used.
7. The trays filled with compost should be covered with the news paper. To increase the moisture of the compost sprinkle water on the paper, not directly on the compost.
8. The casing material should be sterilized first before using for casing. It should be used immediately after making it grem-free. If left for few days it may again be infected.
9. The casing materials must be very fine or it will not effect aeration readily.
10. After spawning and before casing the compost will be watered as needed.

11. If cow manure is used as a casing material the dung should thoroughly decompose in course of a year.
12. After casing the temperature of the room should be 22°-24°C for the first three days. Then it will be reduced to 14°-18 °C.
13. To raise the humidity of the room and to reduce the temperature cold water should be sprayed on the walls. Some prefers to make hessian screens between the tray stacks, which is soaked at noon by sprinkling water on them. Towards the evening those screens are rolled up for the normal air circulation. There are others who like to keep gunny bags filled with moist saw dust. This will increase the humidity of the room.
14. If the casing does not crack on drying aeration does not take place properly. In such case prick the casing at places to break the entirety. If the pin heads do not grow change the casing.
15. If any mould occurs spray fungicide immediately. In case it is not effective remove the affected trays from the room.
16. If watering is needed it should not be done just before picking mushroom.
17. The cavities formed due to picking mushrooms should be filled with the sterilized casing material.
18. Mushroom should not be picked by cutting the stalk, because the disease infection may occur.
19. To clean the room the broom stick should not be used. Because it helps spread germs of diseases in all parts of the room. Therefore, the floor should be cleaned by wiping.
20. To enter the room the shoes should be changed. The slipper kept near the door should be used. This prevents entering the germs from outside.

Delicious Recipies Of Mushroom

MUSHROOM PRAWN CURRY

Ingredients : Mushroom .... 250 g.
Cauliflower.. 250 g.
Tomato .... 100 g.
Prawn (Fresh water/brackish
water/saline water .... 200 g.
Onion.. 150 g.
Salt & chilli.. According to taste
Ghee/Butter/oil .... 5 table spoonfuls.

Cook cauliflower (pieces) and potato (pieces) with oil and keep it apart. Then cook mushroom (minced) and dressed prawn (minced) with onion (minced) and oil.

Melt oil in a pan, mix the two preparations together and tomato (pieces), salt and Chilli (powder) to it. Stir for five minutes. Then add water sufficient to immerse the ingredients in the pan. Boil until thickened to from a mass with gravy.

This recipe is very wholesome and delicious, which is considered a highly suitable item of the dietary for the women in pregnancy and convalescents.

MUSHROOM TOMATO CURRY

Ingredients : Mushroom .... 250 g
Tomato .... 100 g
Onion .... 100 g
Salt & chilli .... according to taste
Ghee/butter/oil .... 3 table spoonfuls.

Wash the mushroom and cut into pieces. Onion and tomato are also cut into pieces. Melt butter in a pan. Put mushroom tomato and onion pieces into the pan. Stir them for 5 minutes. Then add water to immerse the vegetables. Lower the flame of the stove until the vegetable are cooked.

MUSHROOM POLAO

Ingredients : Rice (Besmati) .... 2 cups
Mushroom .... 300 g
Water .... 3 cups
Cumin .... 2 tea-spoonfuls
Ghee/Butter .... 3 table-spoonfuls.

Clean and wash the rice as usual. Cut mushroom into pieces. Melt ghee in a pan on the stove. Then fry cumin and add mushroom to it and stir for few minutes. Add water to boil the mushroom. Then add salt. When water will start boiling add rice to it. Cook until the water is evaporated. Serve before cooling.

MUSHROOM PUDDING

Ingredients : Fresh mushroom .... 500 g
Ghee/butter .... 1/2 table spoon
Wheat flour(*maida*) .... 1 table-spoon
Sugar .... 100 g
Milk .... 1 lt

Wash the mushroom and cut into pieces, then grind them finely. Melt ghee in a pan and fry mushroom with it. Make a suspension of water, milk and flour. Put it in the pan, add sugar and salt after few minutes and stir until it is thickened. Serve hot.

GHUGNI (PULSE-MUSHROOM CURRY)

Ingredients : Gram/Pea(whole) .... 250 g
Mushroom .... 150 g.
Potato .... 150 g.
Onion .... 200 g.
Ginger .... 200 g.
Garlic .... 25 g.
Cumin 2cloves
Salt and chilli .... 2tea-spoonfuls.
Ghee/butter/oil .... 3 table spoonfuls.

Soak the pulse (gram or pea) in water overnight. Boil it in a pressure cooker with potato (pieces) for 10 minutes.

Melt the remaining ghee in a pan. Put onion, ginger, garlic, cumin and chilli (all minced/ground) in it and stir for frying, then add boiled pulse, potato and fried mushroom to it and add water just to immerse the mass. Add salt and cook until thickened to from gravy. It should be borne in mind that the pulse should remain whole till the end.

Some prefers to prepare *ghugni* with minced meat or prawn. To them mushroom *ghugni* will be at par with meat *ghugni* almost in all respects, if not better.

MUSHROOM SOUP

Ingeredients : Fresh mushroom .... 500 g
Butter/ghee .... 5 g
Wheat flour .... 2 table spoonfuls
Salt .... according to taste
Ground spice (Chilli,cinnamon,cardamon) .... 4 g.
Milk .... 1 lt.

Mince the mushroom. Melt ghee in a pan, add mushroom to fry. Then add milk to it and boil for 5-7 minutes. To thicken the milk add a suspension of water and flour (*maida*) to it, and sir for sometime. Boil the liquid for 5 minutes or so. Then add spices and salt to complete the preparation.

MUSHROOM POKORA

Ingeredients : Mushroom (only the caps).... 6

Egg.. 1

Besan (gram flour) .... 10 g

Baking powder .... 1 tea-spoonful

Bread crumbs .... as needed

Salt and chilli.. According to taste

Butter/oil... Sufficient

Beat the egg and add flour, backing powder, salt, chilli powder. Make doughs of 50 g each. Make a hole on a dough. Stuff the hole with mushroom. Close the opening with a little dough. Roll the doughs in bread crumbs.

Melt butter in a pan. Fry the doughs to brown in sufficient oil. Serve hot.

Another process: Beat the egg and add gram flour, backing powder, salt, chilli powder to it. To make a thick batter a little water may be needed to add. Add minced mushroom to the batter. Scoop out a little batter (50 g approx) and roll it in bread crumbs.

Melt butter in a pan. Fry the doughs to brown in sufficient oil. Serve hot with tomato sauce.

MUSHROOM-PEA CURRY

Ingeredients : Mushroom .... 250 g

Green pea.. 250 g

Onion.. 1

Tomato 1

Cumin .... 1 tea-spoonful

Ground spices
(Chilli, cinnamon, cardamon, clove) .... 2 tea-spoonfuls

Salt .... According to taste

Ghee.. as needed

Wash the mushroom and cut into small pieces. Take out the peas from the pods. Melt ghee in a pan on the oven. Add cumin to it. When tossed about add onion (minced), tomato (pieces), peas, mushroom and salt. Cook it in low heat and add a little hot water. When peas will be soft add ground spices to complete cooking.

MUSHROOM SAMOSA (SINGARA)

Ingredients : (for stuffing)

Mushroom.. 250 g

Onion (minced).. 2 bulbs

Green chilli (minced) .... 2 teaspoonfuls

Minced coriender leaf (*Dhania*) .... 1 table-spoonful

Salt (for casing) .... as needed to taste

Wheat flour (*maida*) .... 300 g

Salt... as needed to taste

Ghee... 3 table-spoonfuls.

Mushroom is cut into pieces. Onion is also cut into pieces. Melt ghee in a pan on the oven. Add mushroom, onion, chilli and salt to it and cook for few minutes. When the fluid dries up put off the fire and add *Dhania* to it. It will be used for stuffing.

Make small balls with the dough and roll them into small *chapaties*. Cut each into halves. Take one half and make a triangular case and stuff it with the cooked mushroom. Close the opening and fry them in sufficient ghee. Serve hot with tomato or mustard sauce.

LIVER WITH MUSHROOM

Ingredients : Mushroom (pieces) .... 250 g

Liver (goat/sheep)....................................... 150 g

Tomato 2

Onion... 2 bulbs

Ginger (ground)... 2 tea-spoonfuls

Garlic (ground).. 4 cloves

Chilli (powder) .... 1 tea-spoonful

Salt.. as needed to taste

Ghee/butter/oil .... 3 table-spoonfuls.

Melt ghee in a pan. Fry onion, red to brown. Add ginger, garlic, tomato (pieces), chilli and salt to it and cook for 3-5 minutes. Then add liver (minced), mushroom, tomato (pieces) and cook for 5 minutes, Then add a cup of hot water. Put off the fire when the fluid dries up.

MUSHROOM-PRAWN FRY

Ingredients : Mushroom (pieces) .... 150 g.
Small prawn (Not shrimp) .... 100 g.
Onion (pieces) .... 150 g.
Chilli (powder) .... 1 tea-spoonful
Salt .... as needed to taste
Oil .... 2 table-spoonfuls.

Heat oil in a pan. Fry onion and chilli for 5 minutes. then add mushroom, prawn (minced) and salt to it. Cook for 5-7 minutes.

MUSHROOM OMLET

For an egg omelet one standard size egg is sufficient. One mushroom (without stalk) is minced. Add salt to it Melt ghee in a pan, add mushroom to it. Cook it for 3-4 minutes. Take it from the pan. Pour beaten egg mixed with minced onion and green chilli in the pan. Spread it as usual and scatter fried mushroom on the layer of beaten egg. Roll it as usual and fry both the surfaces (upper and lower) alternately. When fried put off the fire.

MUSHROOM PICKLE

Ingredients : Fresh mushroom .... 500 g
Salt .... 20 g
Ginger (ground) .... 5 g
Mace .... 22 g
Fenugreek (ground) .... 20 g
Red chilli powder .... 10 g
Vinegar .... 3/4 cup
Mustard oil .... 100 g

Soak button mushroom in water for few minutes. Drain off the water. Take clean mushroom pieces, salt, chilli, mace and fenugreek in a porcelain pot.

Heat the oil in a pan. Add ginger to it and cook it to light brown colour. Then put mushroom and spice mixture in the pan. Add vinegar to it and cook for 10 minutes. Put off the fire. After few minutes fill the glass jars with the preparation and put the lid tightly. After a week the pickle can be used.

Commercial Aspects And Economics

Mushroom growing even in the cottage scale is profitable. As the demand has been increased the price in the market is also high. At present the price of the button mushroom is higher than any other mushroom. In the next place stands the paddy-straw mushroom. The third being the oyester mushroom. Its price is comparatively cheap. The black mushroom (*Morchella esculenta*, Guchi) is found growing in Punjab, Kashmir, Chamba, Kumaon hills, the Himalayas and Himachal Pradesh. It is considered a precious food article. In the fresh condition it is sold at Rs. 150-200/kg. It is mainly exported in the dried from to Europe (France and Switzerland) and America and sold there at even Rs. 1500/kg. This is the international market. At present the fresh button mushroom is sold at Rs. 125/kg. The price of the paddy-straw mushroom is Rs. 80-100/kg. The button mushroom preserved in the glass jar or tin container is sold at Rs.270/kg.

THE STATEMENT OF EXPENDITURE AND PROFIT WHEN GROWN IN A SMALL SCALE

A. Recurring cost
(for the two crops in winter under a shed of 20 sq.m.)

i)	Straw 20 quintals @ Rs.80/-quintal	=	Rs.1,600.00
ii)	Wheat bran (*Bhusi*) 100kg. @ Rs.6.00	=	Rs. 600.00
iii)	Fertilizer (Urea 20kg, CAN 15kg)	=	Rs. 250.00
iv)	Gypsum 100 kg. @ Rs.1.50/kg.	=	Rs. 150.00
v)	Pesticides and fungicides	=	Rs.150.00
vi)	Spawn 50 bottles @ Rs.20/bottle	=	Rs.1000.00
vii)	Labour cost Rs.1200 p.m. for 5 months	=	Rs.6,000.00
viii)	Miscellaneous	=	Rs.1,000.00
	Total cost	=	**Rs.10,750.00**

B. Non-recurring Expenditure

i)	Cost of construction of mud house area 20 sq.m. and shelves @ Rs.300/sq.m.	=	Rs.5,400.00
ii)	Cost of equipments (Sprayers, water can, implements)	=	Rs.1,500.00
	Total cost	=	**Rs.6,900.00**

C. Depreciation and interest @ 30% of Rs.6900/- = Rs.2,070.00

D. Expected yield - 500 kg (for two crops)

Estimated turn over from 500 kg @ Rs. 50.00 (Rate of the wholesale market) = Rs.25,000.00

Expenditure

Recurring cost	=	Rs. 10,750.00
Depreciation and interest	=	Rs. 2,070.00
(Not taking into account of nonrecurring cost)	=	Rs.12,820.00

Profit

Expenditure	=	Rs. 12820.00
Expected yield - 500 kg (for two crops)	=	Rs. 25000.00
Profit	=	Rs.12,180/-

Cost of production 1 kg. of mushroom (approx)	=	Rs. 25.64
Net profit per kg. mushroom is nearly	=	Rs. 24.36

Note:

1) If the produce can be sold in the retail market the profit will be double, i.e. (Approx Rs.24,360.00)

2) The compost after use is still a good manure for other agricultural purposes. It can be sold for Rs.500.00-1000.00.

Nutrition From Mushroom

Mushroom is a delicious and nutritious food article. Obviously the food value of fresh and preserved mushroom are not the same. First the fresh mushroom will be discussed in this respect.

The importance of mushroom as a food is for the presence of vitamins and minerals. Protein stands in the second position. But in comparison with other protein-rich food mushroom is most welcome. Because the protein content though not too high the whole of it is digested and assimilated easily in the body. Hence the importance. The protein from the animal sources are costly and as such the sufficient quantity cannot be consumed. The beans and pulses are rich in vegetable proteins. But they are not fully assimilated in our bodies. Hence the wastage. Considering all these it is rightly said, *Mushroom is vegetable meat*.

Mushroom supplies us vitamin B-Complex significantly (0.14 mg/kg). This composite vitamin is not lost due to cooking. Mushroom is an important source of folic acid. It is very useful to the anemic patients. Anemia is a common trouble of the women in pregnancy in the developing countries. So it is imperative to include mushroom in their dietary .Though in traces mushroom contains vitamins A, C, D and K.

Fresh mushroom contains minerals in plenty (0.9-1.7%) which is greater than those of fruits and vegetables (excepting leafy vegetables). Of those salts potassium, phosphorous, copper and iron are main, and other salts are sodium, calcium, magnesium and zinc. The button mushroom contains 0.45% of phosphorous, 0.144% of potassium, 0.11% of sodium, 0.006% of calcium, 1.55 ppm of copper, 18.7 ppm of iron, 13.20 ppm of magnesium and zinc.

The important chemical which helps digest protein is proteolytic enzyme. Meat treated with this enzyme is cooked quickly. Hence the name 'meat tenderizer'. Mushroom contains enough of this enzyme. Those meats which are not cooked easily when mixed with mushroom become tender early. If fish, meal or egg is cooked with mushroom more protein can be available.

Mushroom supplies us less calorie (135 c/kg) than many other foods. Because it does not contain enough carbohydrates. Obviously it is an ideal for the diabetic patient and also for those who are willing to reduce the fat of the body keeping the nutrition intact.

The experiments prove the mushroom can destroy some harmful fungi, bacteria and vires in the body. Not only that it inhibits the tumour growth also. To reduce the plasma cholesterol the two species of mushroom e.g. *A. bisporus* and *Lentimus adades* are recommended as an important food article.

In dried mushroom protein and minerals are more in comparison with its weight. But 60% of vitamin is lost while drying. Due to drying the weight is reduced by 10-13 parts. The dried mushroom can absorb moisture from air readily. Therefore it should be preserved in the air-tight polythene pouches. If preserved so the food value is not lost.

Canned mushroom is very popular in the developed countries. It can be preserved in the same way as practised in case of pickle, jam, Jelly, and *Chatni*. For this reason mushroom is preserved in brine or in butter. To find out the improved technique to preserve mushroom the research works are being carried on in the department of Fruit and Horticultural Technology of ICAR. They recommend to preserve mushroom in common salt (2%), sugar (2%) and citric acid (0.3 parts).

The food value of button mushroom preserved in this way are given below. But in canned mushroom 5-60 per cent of vitamins is lost.

Nutrients (%)	Dried	Canned
Protein	27.4	20.00
Fat	3.9	2.4
Carbohydrates	52.6	49.9
Fibre	6.6	8.3
Ash (minerals)	15.7	12.2
Calorie	337.0	300.0

Mushroom Growing In Gardens

Mushroom grow in their natural habitats. If the favourable condition of their growth are provided they can be grown outdoors. Of them *Agaricus campestris* and *Volvariella volvacea* can be gown easily. The former grows world wide. In the late rains, i.e. in September it is found to grow solitarily or in clusters in the field, pasture, under the bushes and trees of deciduous forest as well as in fallow lands. But never in the evergreen forest. It is very popular as a delicious vegetable.

Though the mushroom growth is strictly seasonal the mycelium of A. *campestries* is perennial, i.e. it always remains in the soil and spread when plenty of humus from rotton roots are obtained. It should be borne in the mind that the mycelium grow in the subsoil. The pin heads growing in the subsoil pass through a soil layer of 30-40 cm. deep before they raise the heads above the soil surface. The stalk above the ground is solid but the lower part of its is hallow.

Select a place near the trees in the garden. It should be borne in mind that the land should not be cultivated. Because it grows in fallow lands near the forest. The species prefers the humus deposited in the sub-soil due to the decomposition of roots.

Make a number of holes of 15 cm diameter and 30cm deep at a distance of 60 cm. Make a mixture of leafmould, diammonium phosphate (DAP) and saw dust at the ratio of 10 : 1 : 10 (by weight). To the mix add a pinch of mushroom spores collected in the process of paper print and mix the ingredient thoroughly. Put two handfuls of the mix in eve of the monsoon. The position of the holes should be marked on the ground. Because the process will be repeated making new holes in the alternate year. The first crop can be obtained after 18 months of the culture. After wards the fruit bodies will be growing from August--October every year. The small weeds, herbs or shrubs, should not be removed from the plot from July to January.

Now it will be discussed how *V. volvacea* (paddy-straw mushroom) can be grown under a tree from the straw waste of the farmyard.

Make a bamboo frame of 3m × 1m size. To make a platform above the ground put the frame horizontally on some stands made with bricks which should be 30cm high.

The process should be started in April. Stack the paddy straw 1m high on the plateform. Before piling soak the straw in water. In dry summer water the stack once a week. In the middle of may scatter DAP on the stack at the rate of 100g per sq.m. After a week apply 200g of *besan* (flour of gram) by sprinkling on the stack. Then after a week sprinkle a pinch of spore on the stack and cover the top with a layer of soaked straw. The mushroom spore can be collected by the process of paper ptint. If the spores are not available use the decomposed straw with mycelium where the mushroom (*Volvariella* sp) has grown. It is better to cover the stack with a nylon netting or the birds, domestic fowls or mongooses may disturb the pile. Secondly to keep it free from the termites and ants use termite killer on the ground especially near the stands of the platform.

Mushroom will begin to grow from the middle of July. After each batch of the crop apply *besan* as before. But no spawn has to be added. From November to March the pin heads would not grow. In April start the process as before on the old pile. The decomposed straw of the previous year should not be removed.

Preservation of Mushroom

Mushroom, like fruit and vegetable, is highly perishable. It grows in profusion at an interval of 8-10 days. If it is preserved the supply can be had in the short gap, lean period or out of season. When the production is high it is imperative to preserve the produce for the market of inland as well as abroad where it has a great demand.

The mushroom can be persevered in a fresh condition for 7 days. In the European countries the fresh mushroom is also sent to the distant market. Button mushroom are packed in a polythene packet and kept in 15-21 °C for sending to the distant market. If kept in a fibre glass tray and covered with another tray the mushrooms can be preserved for 7 days in 1 °C.

Another method is to fill a polythene bag with mushroom and nitrogen gas. If kept in 0 °C it will remain fresh for 5 weeks. But in 5 °C or 15 °C the mushroom will remain fresh for 4 weeks or two weeks respectively. In south India mushroom is put in polythene bags which are carried in bamboo baskets to the markets of a long distance.

FREEZE DRYING

Mushroom is cut into small pieces and soaked in 0.05 per cent brine and sodium metabisulphite for 30 minutes. Then taken out from the solution and put into boiling water for only two minutes. On cooling keep it in 22 °F for a minute. Then put in a freeze drier. On drying preserve it in the vacuum tins. The dried mushroom should not contain more than 3 per cent of moisture. Without canning it can be preserved in a deep freeze. Taking out of the boiling water the mushroom on cooling is put into a deep freeze.

DRYING METHOD

Mushroom is dried in the sun or in a mechanical dehydrator at 60-70 °C. If the stalks are very long they will be cut into small pieces. Then the material will be packed in a air-tight container. The polythene or polyester pouch are suitable for this purpose. If the sealed pouches are kept in a cool place the materials can be preserved for 9-12 months. Thoroughly dried mushroom in a powder from can be preserved in pouches or tins. Powdered mushroom is very suitable for preparing soup.

Another method is to put the mushroom in a boiling water for some time, then the material is dried in 60-70 °C. When thoroughly dried put it in pouches and sealed as usual. To preserve the normal colour and flavour take out the material from boiling water; then on cooling soak it in chlorine solution then treat it with sodium metabisulphite and pack after drying in a freeze drier. In this method mushroom can be preserved with its colour and flavour intact for a year or so.

Another form of preservation is pickling. Mushroom pickle in glass jars or tin containers can be preserved easily even by the housewives. The preparation has been discussed in Chapter 14.

Edible Mushrooms of This Country

In a natural habitat a good number of edible mushrooms grow here in India. Some of them grow in large quantities in the wild. Generally the tribal people collect them from the forest lands and sell in the market. Of them which are delicious fetch a good price. They are available in the market from June to November.

Generally the edible mushrooms belong to two classes. e.g. Basidiomycetes and Ascomycetes. The former includes the family Agaricaecae that comprises the most of the edible species. Its characteristic shape being umbrella-like. The most of the edible species of India are described below.

- ***Agaricus arvensis***: It grows in the cultivated as well as in fallow lands. In gardens as well in pastures it is also found to grow. The top (pileus) is smooth, white or yellowish. The shape is ball-shaped. It grows in the certain places of West Bengal, Gujrat and in the eastern part of Maharastra.

- ***Agaricus bisporus***: It grows on the manure heaps. In the first stage of growth the head is conves and then it becomes flat. The colour is white which turns grey, and at the last becomes brown. It is found to grow in Solan (H.P.)

- ***Agaricus campestris***: This species is widely known. The regional names of this species are "Khumbi" (Hindi), Kanrdal Chhatu"; "Parban Chhatu"; "Durga Chhatu" (Bengali); "Kukkagodugu" (Tel); "Khumb" (Punjab). It is found to grow in all parts of the country, especially in the plains and hills of North-East India. In the plains it grows in September-october. It grows where humus is present in the subsoil. The stalk is white, smooth and solid, and very long as it rises from the subsoil. The cap is round and then convex, and at the last is flat. Gills are white that turns pink to purple or brown. In the final stage they become almost black.

- ***Cantharellus cibarius***: The regional names are *Dhingri* (Punjab); *Simote* (Santal). The cap is 5-8 cm in diameter, the colour is yellowish. It is a mushroom of the low hills of north-east India. It grows in the humus-rich sandy soil. The cap is convex, then flat and at the last it becomes concave. The gills are thick and vein-like.

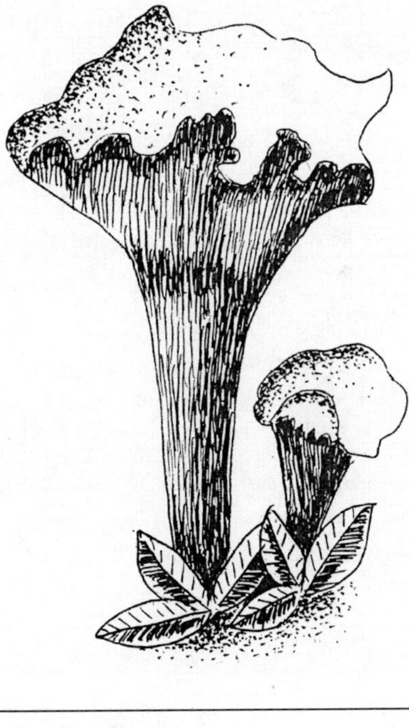

Fig. 20: *Cantharella cibarius*

- ***Agaricus praecox***: In bushes, pastures and fallow lands this species is found to grow. In the early stage the cap is convex and then becomes flat, the colour is off white which turns yellowish to brown in the later stage. The periphery of the cap is curved inward and lately upward. Sometimes on the top small cavities are formed. It is found to grow in Saharanpur (U.P.)
- ***Amanita caesaria***: This species has two varieties. One of them is orange, large in size and attractive. The top is smooth and hemispherical. When full-grown it becomes flat, the border is bent inwards. The colour is red or orange, and yellow towards the margin. The veil on the stalk hangs downwards. It is found to grow in Baroda (Gujarat) and in the Khasi hills.
- ***Armillaria mellea***: It grows solitarily or in clusters. It not only grows in soil but also on the stumps of trees. The head is fleshy and of honey colour. The margin is marked with lines. The centre of the cap is deep brown. It is found to grow in certain places in Gujarat and Uttar Pradesh.
- ***Bovista plumbea***: It is a very small mushroom that grows in fallow lands. In a hot weather just after the rain it grows in profusion. It does not develop rhizoids for anchoring. For this reason the full-grown mushroom fall off on the ground. The colour is off-white. The top is very smooth. It is found to grow in Aligarh, Mussouri, Sonamarg, Khardrala etc.
- ***Coprinus micaceus***: It is mainly grows on the base of the trees, dead or live. Sometimes on the logs or stumps. In ground it grows in a cluster. The head is oval. On the pin head mica-like scales are found. It is found in south Begal, Nagpur and Shrinagar.
- ***Heterobasidion annosum***: It is grown on the base of the stump, logs and the forest of conifers. The head is large without stalk. The colour is grey to brown, rarely blackish. In the fresh condition it is hard and cork-like. In the dried condition it is like wood, i.e. hard and long-lasting. It is found in U.P., Assam and Punjab, and in certain places of Himachal Pradesh.
- ***Hydnu sepandum***: The head is yellowish and white, as if the skin of a deer. Hence its name *Doeskin mushroom*. The size and colour is unstable. It grows solitarily or in clusters. The top is fleshy, brittle and convex and flat. The margin is often wavy. The colour is yellowish to black-red. The flesh is white. The bruised point becomes brown. The taste is good with

sweet scent. It grows it certain places in Uttar Pradesh and Himachal Pradesh.

- ***Macrolepiota mostoida***: It grows in the field. In the early stage of growth it is ball-shaped. Then becomes convex. The colour is white. The brown or grey scale are found to grow on the top. It grows in certain places of Calcutta, Hooghly and Uttar Pradesh.
- ***Macrolepiota procera***: It is found to grow in gardens, forests or bushes. The cap is thin and covered with brown scales. The stalk is very long and hollow towards the bottom. The veil is thick and hard. It becomes loose in the later stage of growth. It is found mainly in Calcutta, Lucknow and Saharbnpur.
- ***Morchella esculenta***: It is found to grow in the forest, road side, old apple or peach orchard. The head is oval and like an half-open umbrella. The centre is blunt, i.e. not conical. It is found in Punjab, Kashmir, Chamba, Kumaun and Himachal Pradesh.

Fig. 21: *Morchella esculenta*

- ***Pleurotus sajor-caju***: It is well known oyester mushroom. It is found in the district of Hooghly, in Andamans and the foot hills of the Himalayas.
- ***Podabrella microcarpa***: Very small and is found to grow in profusion on the mound above the termite nest. The head is small, flat and smooth.

The margin is pink in colour. This species is found in many places of West Bengal and Tamil Nadu.

- ***Russula emitica***: It is found to grow in the field or forest in solitarily or in clusters. It also grows on decaying wood. Head is brittle. A milk-like liquid oozes from a broken point. In the first stage it is ball-shaped, then convex and in the last stage it becomes concave. The colour of the pin head is pink to red which turns dull afterwards. The cap is smooth, glossy and sticky. Not so delicious. It is found in Darjeeling and Khasi hills. it is also identified as a poisonous species.

- ***Lycoperdum bovista***: It is also known as *Giant puff ball* : The regional names are *Boenfal* (Punjab); *Horputica* (Santal).

  Large in size, off-white and flat. The lower side is folded or furrowed. The mycelium grows in bundles and serves as a thick root. In summer just after the rains it is found to grow in pastures and under the trees or bushes. When it turns yellow it should not be eaten. In other countries it is very popular.

- ***Volvareilla deplosia***: It is also known as *paddy-straw mushroom*. it grows mainly in the coastal regions, especially in West Bengal, Orissa and Tamil Nadu. The stalk is 6-12.6 cm long, white and the base is bulb-like. Head is umbrella-like, the margin is serrated. The gills are white which turns off white or creamy.

  This mushroom is very soft and delicious. In the rains it grows on the piles of decomposed straw in the farmyard. It is grown widely in Thailand and China. For its culture spawn is now available in West Bengal and Tamil Nadu.

- ***Volvariella terastria***: It is also a 'paddy-straw Mushroom' which grows on the decomposed straw heaps.

- ***Volvariella volvacea***: It is the largest species of the genus *Volvariella*. The stalk is also proportionately long. The colour is grey to brown. In West Bengal it grows widely on the decomposed paddy-straw heaps in the rains. It is very soft and delicious. Hence the popularity.

Poisonous Mushrooms

The poisonous species are not more in numbers in fungi. Of them few look likes the edible mushroom. Therefore the poisonous species are not easily distinguishable. So it is imperative to eat those species which are known as edible. There are however some mushrooms that lose their poison to a great extent in the process of cooking.

- ***Amanita phalloides:*** it is a very common mushroom that causes 90 per cent of the total deaths caused by the poisonous mushroom. Some persons of the several families of Assam died due to the mushroom poison. It is assumed that the responsible species being A. *phalloides*. Its stalk (Stipe) is 10-12 cm long with a tinge of yellow and green colour, the Veil is very conspicuous, white or greenish. The top is fleshy, first round and then flat. The colour is off white, yellowish or brown. The gills are thick, i.e. more numerous and white. its poisonous effect is due to the presence of the poisonous chemicals like phalloidine, A-Amatine and B-Amatine. The former is a poison of liver.
- ***Amanita muscaria:*** It is a common poisonous mushroom. The stalk is 20-25 cm long. It grows on the medium altitude of the hills. The cap is of 15-25 cm in diameter, and bright red and glossy. Some warty growths are found on the top. The stalk is white or yellowish, solid and straight.

Sometimes scaly, gills are thick. The border is finely serrated, white or yellowish in colour. In Russia it is used as the fly killer. To attract the flies it is mixed with the strong syrup. It has three poisonous chemicals. These are cholin, muscarine and mycetoatropine.

Fig. 22: *Amanita phlloides.*

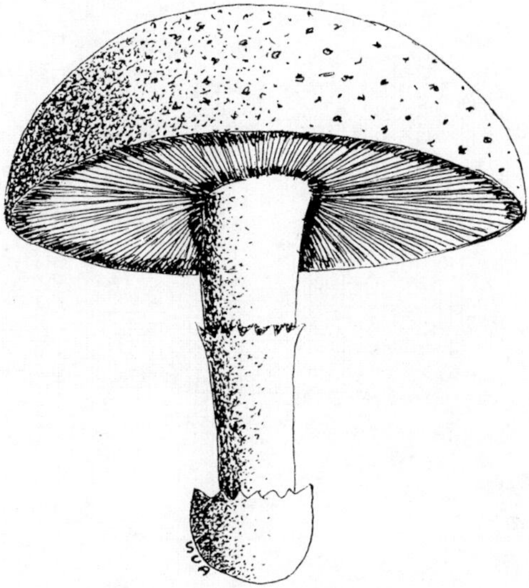

Fig. 23: *Amanita muscaria*

Other less poisonous mushroom are *Russla emitica, Panaeolus* spp., *Gyromitra esculenta, Stropharia semiglobata, Hypholoma fasciculare, Lacterius vellerius, Dictophora phaloeda, Lepiota cristata* and *Marasmius urens*.

- ***R. emitica:*** It grows in Darjeeling and Khasi range. Its poison damage the stomach and intestine. Vomiting and stomach trouble are the symptoms of poisoning. Muscarine being the poison.
- ***G. esculenta:*** The poisoning symptoms are the stomach trouble and jaundice. This poison causes damage to the red-blood corpuscles. The patient is treated by the transfusion of blood.
- ***Panaeolus* spp:** Some species of this genus have been identified as poisonous. Its poison affects the brain. The patient fails to maintain balance while walking. The eye sight is also affected.
- ***S. Semiglobata:*** It grows in the Khasi gange.
- ***H. fascicularia:*** It is found growing in Darjeeling and Simla.
- ***L. vellereus:*** It grows in Sikkim.

- ***D. phaloidea:*** It is found to grow in Sikkim, Khasi range, North Bengal and Mumbai.
- ***M. urens:*** It has also been identified as a poisonous species.
- ***L. cristata:*** Its head is not like that of common mushroom. The formation is cristate.

Other Uses of Mushroom

Mushrooms have many uses besides the food article. Now-a-days in the forest land of the developed countries the favourable conditions for mushrooms are created. Because in the modern natural science the mushroom is considered an important ecological agent. In other words, to maintain the ecological balance not only green plants but also the mushrooms have their significant roles. For example, the trunks of the dead trees take a long time to decompose in a normal condition. But when attached by the mycelium, growth of mushroom is changed to organic residues within a few years. The leaves fallen off from the trees decompose to form humus. The mycelium of mushroom in the process of absorbing food brings about further changes in them.

In many important industries the use of mushrooms are found. But those are minute. The large-sized mushrooms have very limited use in the industry. There are two species namely *Fomes fomentarius* and *Gonoderma applanatum* from which a suede-like substance is obtained. The suede is used to make costlier garments and other articles like dresses, caps, hand bags, picture frames etc. The tissues of *Polyporus squasmosus* is like a cork which is used to make the lids of bottle and stop-cocks. At present it is used as a strop for sharpening razors. There are many other mushrooms from which many colouring matters are obtained. *Polyporus sulphurus* and *Fomes ignarius* are used to prepare yellow and blackish brown colour respectively. In the foregoing chapter. *Amantia muscaria* has been described as poisonous mushroom. In Russia it is used as a poison to kill flies. It is mixed with a concentrated syrup to attract the flies. *Amantia muscaria* acts as a stimulant like a drug that creates hallucination and forgetfulness. If a man eats this mushroom his memory is lost and he forgets his own identity. Fortunately the responsible chemical does not stay in the body, it is excreted with urine without undergoing any changes.

Then the patient becomes normal. Some species of *Stropharia* and *Psilocybe* genera have the similar characters. *Psilocybe* contains Psilocybin and Psilocin which are used to cure mental disease. *Daedalea quercika* is used as a comb to rub the body of a horse. It is also used as a comb to clean the hair of man. *Polyporus formenlarius* is also known a *Tinder mushroom*, because it is used as tinder of the cigar light. It catches fire by the sparks of the stone. If mushroom tinder is used, ciger lights do not need petrol or gas. If oak trees are attacked by *Chlorosplenium aeruginosum* a nice green stain marks their wood, and that wood has a great demand for fashionable woodworks.

The hanging baskets for scandent indoor plants are made from some species of large mushroom. *P. formentarius* or *P. ignitatius* are used for the purpose. Cut off the tube-like structure and hold its convex side upwards. Thus it will look like a flowerpot. Writing ink is prepared from the *Coprinus comatus*. On picking keep the mushroom in a glass pot. Gradually it will fuse to from ink.

In the darkness many lower animals, plants and bacteria radiate the rays of light. In the deep forest the mycelium grown on the stump radiates light. This species is *Ormilaria melia*. When a dead tree attacked by the mycelium of this species the radiation of lights takes place. its mycelium can absorb moisture from the air and as such the infected area always remain moist. Illuminated trees or stumps serve as the light house to the forest guards passing the forest in the dark night. In the mines *Fomes anosus* grows. The mycelium and fruit bodies of this species illuminate. The light is radiated from the gills of *Pleurolus japonicus*. The intensity of light radiated by a mushroom can help read the Roman alphabets of 5mm. size. One can read a book in the illumination from the mushroom species *Boletus edulis* and *B. calibia*. 'Aagerick' is efficacious against many diseases and is prepared from a mushroom *Polyporus officinalis*. Previously this mushroom was taken as a purgative. No other purgative was so efficacious as this mushroom. Hence the popularity. To stop bleeding from an injury it was applied as a blam. It is also expectorant to clear of phlegm from the chest and lungs. To stop the perspiration of the tuberculosis patient at night it is efficacious too. it is taken as a food to control gout, pleurisy, jaundice and the thread worms of the intestine. Homeopathy medicines like 'Boletus laricis', 'Agaricus albus' etc. are prepared from this mushroom.

Auricularia auricula is used as a blam to cure the swelling of eyes. Add is used as a mouth wash to cure the swelling of the throat. The blood is clotted quickly at the point of haemorrhage by the use of *Fomes ignarius* and *F. fomentarius*. *Lycoperdon giganteum* is used as a soft dressing for injuries. Even to day *Clavitia gigantia* is to cause anesthesia. Since the ancient times the powder or decoction of *Amanita muscaria* is used to cure gland swelling, epilepsy etc. Homeopathy medicine 'Agaricus muscarius' is prepared from this mushroom. It is also a medicine to cure heart trouble and gout.

Volvariella volvacea and *Flammulina velutipes* can be used to reduce the high blood pressure and the growth of tumor cells. The curative medicines against certain types of cancer and influenza virus have been found in mushrooms. On discovery of the antibiotic penicillin from *Penicillium*, it appears to be promising for such more discoveries leading to the cure of many deadly diseases. It is reported that the success have been achieved to find out some medicines against the cancer.

Appendices

A

PANORAMA

It has been mentioned already that the production and the use (as a food article) of mushroom are more in Himachal Pradesh than the other parts of the country. Now-a-days the importance has been laid on mushroom growing in Rajasthan more than ever. To make it popular there the contribution of the scientists of the agricultural university is greater than that of the others. There they have arranged to impart training among the villager regularly. They being invited by the Gujarat Royal Technical Institute and in auspices of Alembic Limited (Boroda) arranged training on mushroom growing. As a result, the demand of mushroom and mushroom spawn has increased there greatly.

There are a number of tourist centres in Rajasthan which attracts many tourists of home and abroad. For this reason the standard hotel industry has developed in those centrs. In the hotels mushroom preparations have occupied a significant place in the menus. Of them lake palace, Shikarvadi, Rajdarshan and Laxmibilas of Udaipur, Umed Bhawn of Jodhpur, Clerk Ameer and Hotel Mansingh of Jaipur are to name. In an observation made in 1991 it is found that the demand of mushroom in these hotels was nearly one tonne per month. The local people also have taken mushroom as a delicious food. As a result, the demand outside the hotels was estimated to be one tonne. In other words the total demand of mushroom in the state of Rajasthan was (in 1991) two tonnes. In every year that demand increases atleast by 10 per cent. So as per this rate the present demand being 3.5 tonnes per month. The eighty per cent of this demand are met with the produce of the local mushroom growers and the natural sources, mainly from the forest land. And the rest (20%) is coming from the outside of the state in packets or from the other countries. Of the local mushroom growers whose production were highest in 1991 are Indreswar Enterprise of Udaipur (200kg per month), Mahalaxmi Mushroom (150kg) and Jadav Nursery of Udaipur (100kg per month).

In West Bengal, the popularity of mushroom is not so as expected. The reasons lie in that the production in the eastern region of the country is less and the people there are not so aware of its food value. Very few of them know that nothing can compete with mushroom as a source of vegetable protein. No other vegetable protein is so easily digested and assimilated in the body. It is an ideal food for anemic patients as well as for those who have got beriberi, diabetes and heart troubles. To reduce the harmful cholesterol, blood sugar and high blood pressure no food can equal mushroom.

There may be a great demand in Calcutta alone. At present its use is limited mainly in big hotels and restaurants. They use mushrooms preserved in packets or other containers. With a view to meeting the demand of Calcutta two firms have started the production of button mushroom. One of them is N.P.C. Mushroom which has started a farm on 16 acres of land at Raspunj of Bhakhra hat (Calcutta). It uses the air conditioned rooms to control the temperature and humidity for the year-round production of button mushroom. The second firm is Transvalley Food Private Ltd. of Kurseong. In this firm 1460kg of button mushroom is produced from 5 tonnes of compost. The full produce preserved in packets is marketed in Calcutta. At present N.P.C. Mushroom produces one tonne of button mushroom a day. This firm is aiming at the foreign markets. Of them Singapur shows a great prospect. It is not too far from Calcutta. Secondly there the demand of mushroom is extremely great. The production of these two firms however large it may be, will not be able to meet the full demand expected in the near future in the eastern region of the country. So to meet this large demand we need numerous small or cottage scale growers distributed all over the area. As the produce from the kitchen gardens meet the significant part of our total vegetable demand, to meet the total demand of mushroom we need the extensiveness of mushroom culture by the cottage growers.

Button mushroom preserved in glass jars and tin containers are available in the New market at Lindsay Street in Calcutta. 220 grams of button mushroom preserved in a glass jar with water, salt and citric acid is sold at Rs.60.00. It is packed by ELMAC, Calcutta -16. Another firm has canned 220 grams of button mushroom with water, salt and citric acid, which is sold at Rs. 54/-. The name of the second firm being Alpha Foods & Chemical Pvt. Ltd. Calcutta-53.

B

SOURCES OF SPAWN

1. Mycology Division, IARI, Pusa, New Delhi-12.
2. Agricultural Research Institute, Loli Rd, Coimbatore.
3. Mushroom Research Centre, Agricultural Complex, Himachal Pradesh University, Solan, Himachal Pradesh.
4. Bidhan Chandra Krishi Viswavidyalaya, Mohanpur, Nadia.
5. State Agricultural Research Institute, 237, Netaji Subhas Rd., Regent Park, Calcutta-40.
6. assistant pathologist, Chinsura Rice Research Centre, Hooghly.
7. Bibha Enterprises (India), Rabindra Nagar, Midnapur, Pin-721 101.

C

BIBLIOGRAPHY

1. A Hand book on Mushroom - Nita Bahl.
2. Edible Mushroom and their cultivation - Chang
3. Manual of Indian Edible Mushroom - Singh.
4. Mushroom - ICAR, New Delhi-12
5. Mushroom : Pest and disease control - Fletcher.
6. Mushroom : The art of cultivation - Singh.
7. Mushroom for Livelihoob - Vijya.

8. Mushroom Growing of Today - Atkins, F.C.

9. Mushroom Production and Processing Technology, Pathak V. N., Agro Botanica, 4E 176 J. N. Vyas Nagar, Bikaner 334 003 (India).

10. Science and Cultivation of Edible Fungi (A set of 2vols) - Elliot.

11. Text book of Fungi - Gupta.

D

SCIENTIFIC PAPERS

1. Agarwal, R.K. 1993- How to grow Mushroom ? Indian journal of Mushroom 1 (!) : 17-21.

2. Alicbusan, R.V. 1979 - Mushroom Production Technology for Rural Development - Food and Nutrition Bulletin Supplementary, 2nd Nov. 1979, p.p. 99-104.

3. Block, S.S 1965 - Garbage Composting for Mushroom Production, Applied Microbiology 13:5-9.

4. Bose, S.R. 1921 - Possibilities of Mushroom industry in India by Cultivation, Agric. J. India 16:643-647.

5. Chang, S.T. 1987, World Production of Cultivated Edible Mushroom in 1986. Mush. Jour for the Tropics. 7:117-120.

6. Duggar, B.M. 1905 - Some Principles in Mushroom Growing and Spawn Making. W.S. Dept. Agric. Tech. Bull 85: 1-60.

7. Hu, K.J. and N. Liu, 1907 - Study on Granular Spawn. Mush. Sci.8: 275-283.